Gap Year

Lessons From a One-Way Ticket

David Pressley

Gap Year

Copyright © 2022 by David Pressley

All rights reserved.

Book design by David Pressley

Edited by Hannah Pressley - hannahpressley.com

Author photo by Cameron Carnes - cameroncarnes.com

Cover design by nskvsky

Formatted by Michael Davie - grimhousepub.com

Printed in the United States of America

First Printing 2022

First Edition 2022

ISBN: 978-0-578-37122-1

The events in this book have been recalled to the best of the author's ability, although some names and details have been changed to protect the privacy of individuals.

To my wife, Hannah, and my daughter, Emma. And to all who believed in me and supported me in Ukraine.

Contents

Prologue
**God doesn't use only special people for His glory,
He uses me too.**

As I look back at my childhood, I don't see any clues pointing towards a desire to do anything extraordinary. The phrase "Gap Year" didn't exist in my vocabulary. I was born in Georgia into a middle-class family, and my upbringing was relatively normal. I was content with my family's life. It seemed to be routine, and I don't remember dreaming about wanting something different.

I was never the kid out in the woods trying to find new civilization, and I didn't organize grand adventures. Sports weren't my thing; instead, I was in the Boy Scouts for a while. I even won first place in the backward race for wooden toy cars, which isn't quite the hallmark trait of a "cool" kid. I was a pretty nerdy guy.

I was mostly content with being in my bedroom—alone. My mind was a playground of its own, and I primarily used it to carefully design and construct buildings out of Legos. The world existed without limitations or borders in my mind, and I could create what I desired while being in isolation in my bedroom. Having many friends didn't make much sense; I always believed a small group would do just fine. Being at the center of attention was never something I aspired to. I was more of a spectator kind of guy.

My parents were married and lived in the same house with me, my younger brother, and my older sister. My father worked for a bank, and my mother was a school teacher by trade but chose to stay at home with the children when we were younger. As my dad focused on his career, my mom focused on our family. Both parents loved us kids, but they showed it in different ways. I was fortunate.

Neither of my parents were world travelers, and we didn't take many family vacations. Instead, I remember going with my dad each week to take the trash to the local dump. Our routine outing was a little sense of adventure even though we did it the same way each week.

My family lived in the same neighborhood as my grandparents in the outskirts of Atlanta. I enjoyed being only a short bike ride away from them, and I often peddled to their house. My granddad was always tinkering with something in his garage, and the bike I rode was one of his works of art.

I felt the duty to ride to his house often to show him, and the neighborhood, my pride in his craftsmanship. I felt at ease picking up speed on the bike my grandfather built for me because I knew he put his all into the design and manufacturing stages. When I rode towards his house, the wind enveloped me and reminded me of his loving embrace. Being on my bike provided a connection between my granddad and me, and it always made me smile.

Like many kids in their infancy of riding bikes, I was more than once terrorized by a dog who saw my swift passing as an intrusion upon their sacred yard. These occurrences often interrupted the triumphant pride I had in my grandfather's work, but I never let on to the fact. My grandparents encouraged bravery and taking what life threw at me in stride, so I often kept quiet about the near-death experiences I encountered on my journey. Regardless of what I experienced on my bike ride, I always arrived cheerful and courageous.

Although my grandparents took trips to foreign places every few years, they didn't dwell on those experiences. Our conversations rarely involved distant lands. It was clear they loved to travel and had planned their retirement years to do just that. Their love of adventure didn't consume them, and they didn't feel the need to tell me about their plans when they saw me. My ear had a natural inclination to tune in when they discussed their adventures, but I had to poke and prod to hear the stories I desired.

All of the people around me seemed pretty normal. I can't remember any safari tour guides or European backpackers who had any influence on my life. The people who lived in my neighborhood were ordinary nine to five workers who savored the five part more than the nine part. I examined the people around me with an inquisitive nature and wondered why they lived the way they did. I couldn't point to anything wrong or out of place at an early age, but I wondered why they didn't live more exciting lives.

Halfway through the sixth grade, my dad sat our family down and explained his job had offered him a promotion. The change would be advantageous for our family financially, but it meant we had to move cities and states, he explained. We didn't have to move far, only from Atlanta to Birmingham, about 150 miles away. In my young mind, that was forever away. This news devastated my siblings and me, and we cried and pleaded for a different option when our parents broke the news.

For a kid who spent most of his time in his bedroom, the thought of moving to a different state completely disoriented me. Going beyond my grandparents' house felt like an adventure, and I couldn't fathom moving to a different state. Moving didn't make sense in my mind, and I questioned my parents' motives. After all, we had a house a bike ride from grandparents, food on the table, and stability inside the four walls of our Georgia home. The decision felt selfish, and I resented my parents for making it. As a kid, I didn't care about our family having more money or opportunities. In my world, we had all we needed.

I couldn't help feeling the decision my parents had made was a heartless one. It was obvious the kids didn't want to move, but we were powerless to change the outcome. It wasn't long after my parents broke the news when we had a moving truck outside of our home, and a "sold" sign in our front yard. The sign sold not only my family's house but also my sense of stability. I hated that sign.

My family's move happened right after the Twin Towers fell, and although I couldn't articulate it then, I sensed the world was chaotic and uneasy. I think that affected me. The news and images coming from my television set were just as confusing and hectic as my life felt at the time. I didn't know the word for "trauma" then, but it's what I experienced. No matter what my desires were, it was clear my parents had decided to move, and it was up to me to figure out how to deal with it.

As I get older, I realize how nostalgia plays a significant role in my happiness and satisfaction. As an adult, I often look back to the "good times" even though I'm aware today has the potential to be what I look back at in just a few short years. This cycle can be annoying because it feels like I'm not enjoying the present day. I'm thankful I've learned to recalibrate my mind's focus when it begins to drift backward, but it remains a constant battle.

I carried this same nostalgic sentiment as a kid, although not as consciously. Having the mindset of not wanting anything to change, I brought a disposable film camera to school on my last day in Georgia. I carefully charted out what I wanted to remember most and planned to photograph each person and room I desired to keep in memory. My P.E. teacher, bus driver, and Spanish classroom, where a Hispanic friend of mine slipped me authentic Mexican candy, all made the cut. I'm sure I looked creepy walking around my school snapping photos of people and places, but I still have those photos to this day, and they make me smile when I see them. I'm not sure if this act was the catalyst for my still present passion for photography and memories, but it certainly had some degree of impact.

Once I had my photos back from the developer at my local CVS drugstore, I put them in a box with the intent to visit those memories at will. It was a strange time in my life. I knew then I was acting as a historian, but I also had to look towards the future. The disposable camera was teaching me I didn't have to let go of my memories altogether, but I did have to learn to organize them in the timeline of my life. In some ways, it's the same reason I'm writing this book—to remember.

Looking back, I see how my mind was working out how to understand the changes in my life. Each bright flash and shutter click served as a book-end to a chapter in my life. My right index finger clamped my camera's shutter release signifying a physical departure from my previous surroundings. Still, I wasn't yet ready to let go. My heart remained in Georgia even though my bed was now in Alabama.

The move to Alabama was painful. I became more isolated as a kid, maybe even slightly depressed. The world around me seemed less stable, and I second-guessed any attachment I felt to people or places. My hesitations were not a conscious thought; instead, my reluctance was born from insecurity and anxiety. My instinctual response was to question everything and create distance from things that could be taken from me.

My peer relationships in my hometown had begun to

blossom too. Although I enjoyed being alone most of the time, I had started forming more enduring friendships with kids at school and in the neighborhood around the time of the move. At this point in my childhood, I began having friends over to spend the night, and they'd invite me to their homes as well. It felt more like deliberate relationships were forming, not just classroom friendships.

The move seemed to take the social structure right out from under me and replaced it with a blank slate. I didn't understand it. I enjoyed building with Legos in my room, but I didn't want to rebuild relationships. For a kid like me, relationships weren't easy, and they often felt like hard work. Being an introvert has its frustrations, and I saw the move as another obstacle in front of me.

There's no way I could have known it at the time, but the plucking from my Georgia home to my Alabama one changed my mindset on places and surroundings. My grandparents, who used to be a quick bike ride down the street and a big part of my life, were now a full-scale car trip away with at least one stop for more fuel. I didn't understand the situation. It didn't make sense that my parents would make such a drastic change in our lives while knowing their kids didn't want to move.

I'd be lying if I didn't confess my change in mindset didn't come at the cost of anger and frustration. There was a several-year stretch when I hated living anywhere but my hometown. I intentionally put up barriers blocking any real friendships to form, and my relationship with my parents suffered for a short while.

Luckily, I found a way around my social and family hurdles within a year of moving to Alabama, and I met a group of guys who are still my best friends today. In fact, we all take an annual trip specifically designed for adventure and risk of failure. We intentionally set out yearly to primitively camp in a national park to embrace potential pain and misery with the promise of being there for each other no matter the events or outcome.

Many of my friends today are also transplants from other states. We talk daily and have stories that are more than fifteen years old. I'm sure I would have continued to form meaningful friendships in Georgia, but I'm blessed to have the friends I met in Alabama. Regardless of past potentials, I've been fortunate in who I call "friend." My social net is cast a short distance, but I allow it to sink deep. I'm happy with the way my social nature has shaped the way I relate and interact with the world.

In retrospect, I realize my parents were looking beyond a horizon I could see as a kid. They understood opportunities for our family existed in greater magnitude outside of my home-town. As I assess the lives of the people I knew in Georgia, it's now clear how my family's move to Alabama afforded me greater opportunities. Many of my peers in Georgia weren't able to attend college or get jobs that afford their families what I can now offer mine. That doesn't make them any worse than me because there are certainly things to strive for in life besides higher education and financial freedom. Many of the people I knew have loving families of their own and live happy lives. I don't consider myself any better off than them in success or fulfillment, but I now see what my parents saw.

I used to see a lot of value in the stability of my surround-ings, but as I've grown up, my mindset has drastically changed. As an adult, I now realize I thrive in changing environments. I need a certain amount of healthy chaos around me to feel ener-gized or maybe even distracted from my tendencies of isolation. I have to be careful not to surround myself with unnecessary tasks simply to feel busy, but I benefit from constant motion.

I frequently tell my wife, Hannah, I'd rather be busy than bored, but I'm pretty sure I didn't come up with that line. Even to this day, if I don't plan at least a rough outline of projects to be completed on my off-days from work, I find myself feeling stir-crazy and a bit depressed. Alone time is something I still cherish, but I've found myself becoming more of a social observer in the last several years. I want to understand people and their motivations, and sometimes that means staying quiet and observing in group situations. I'm still not the life of the party, and I don't think I ever will be.

Since my move from Georgia to Alabama, I have moved several times in fairly drastic ways. Whether it was to and from Ukraine— what this book is about—or to two other states, adventure has filled my adult life. Along the way, I've learned from many fascinating people. I've been in situations and careers which stretch my introverted mind, and I've learned to love traveling to new places. I suppose my mind linked the disposable film camera I used during my last days in Georgia to exciting new places and adventures because, to this day, I find myself with a camera in my hand more often than not.

Oddly, the semi-traumatic move as a kid from Georgia to Alabama has made me quick to entertain the idea of uprooting. There is something liberating about being willing to say, "I'll go." I've been fortunate enough to be able to say that very phrase multiple times in my professional and personal life. The great thing is, each time I've said, "I'll go," I've been met with exciting experiences and some challenging ones, but I've grown each iteration.

My adult mind has developed the intense desire to wander and not feel particularly tied down to any one place or set of circumstances. I've been blessed with a wife who is always supportive and often reminds me to keep my eyes on the path, although I can't always clearly see the road ahead. My wife and I joke that as soon as I get settled in a new place, I begin the conversation of moving somewhere else. Each time I bring up the notion of a move, she cautiously laughs as she looks to me for some sign of me dismissing my idea as a prank. Without her, I don't think I'd have the necessary safety net for when I start looking up one-way plane tickets to places I've never been. In fact, without her, my wanderlust might become toxic. She's a good anchor.

Throughout this book, I often mention another anchor of mine: Jesus. I want to be upfront about my relationship with Him. It's not a perfect relationship (read that as "I fail often, but God is good"). I won't point you to my life as a blueprint for yours, but I hope to have a few things to share with you, which will point you towards Him.

I know there's at least one of you rolling your eyes right now and ready to put this book down because you've decided this whole Jesus thing is for crazy people. You should also know part of my goal in writing this book is to provide a launch point for you to say, "I'll go," even if it's for something unrelated to Jesus. If there is anything I've learned in the short thirty years I've had on Earth, it's there's more to life than what is prescribed to us. That's all I've needed to realize I have to go, and maybe that's enough for you too.

Don't be surprised when your attempt at your "thing" encounters pushback and uncertainty. I've told you about a few of my setbacks and frustrations as a kid, and there's more to tell, but the reality is you should expect setbacks of your own. Some of these setbacks will be a simple "no" to a question you wanted a "yes" to, and others may be a complete derailment of your plans. That's alright. Keep moving forward. Set your sights on the horizon and keep going.

You may realize the people who question your motives want a more exciting and moving life for themselves. Forget about them for now. People like them aren't worth spending time and energy worrying over. Love them well and be a good example for them, but move on.

When we attempt something significant or courageous or meaningful, there's a lot of room for things to go wrong. Let this motivate you. Nobody gets excited about the mundane areas of life. We know the way to work or school, and we know the things we do in our daily routine. None of these things excite us because we expect them, and they become tired and predictable. When you move from a life no different than your friends, family, classmates, or coworkers towards one filled with whimsy, purpose, and drive, you're going to confront setbacks. I guarantee it. But, a life aimed at achieving your goals and aspirations will rejuvenate you, and it will prove worthwhile.

My hope is people from all walks of life will pick up this book. Some of you may be a kid like I was when my journey began. Others have settled into familiar routines and surroundings as an adult. I'm not going to pretend life doesn't provide certain limitations or obligations, but I also know God made each of us with a unique purpose and design.

Your story will likely not look like mine, and I won't try to imitate yours. But together, we can spur one another on to express our fullest potential in whatever God has called us to. As you read this book, allow your mind to wonder. When a place, a person, or an adventure creeps into your mind, jot it down in a notebook or on these pages. I would be thrilled if my words sparked your next project, idea, or journey. Don't believe you have to go to a distant land to make a difference. Your passion and purpose may be inside your own home or just down the street from you. That's alright.

There's not much incentive I can give you if you're dead set on staying where you are. I don't fault you if that's you but just know ahead of time this book probably isn't for you. But, who knows, maybe this book is precisely what you are looking for if you want to change your outlook on your place in the world. I ask whether you finish this book or don't make it past this page please don't put it on your bookshelf when you're finished reading. As you read, think of who might benefit from these words and give this book to them once you're finished. If you're like my wife, you will cover these pages in highlighter marks and notes, but don't let that stop you from gifting it to someone else.

As I sit here and write these words years after moving back to the States, I hope you see the joy and whimsy of what nine short months of commitment to a crazy idea can do for you. Since moving back to America, I've graduated from college, been successful in two different careers, gotten married, and moved to two other states. But, you know what? I still often think back to my time in Ukraine and begin to smile. I talk to my wife, probably more than she cares for, about that period of my life as I start to daydream of my next adventure.

It's time to get started on your journey. Find something you are passionate about, or even good at, and commit a certain amount of time and energy to chase the dream you let go of years ago. As I graduated high school, my dream was to move across the world to help little orphaned kids and grow in love myself. Now, my goal is for you to seriously consider and act on my call to action.

You have what it takes inside of you to accomplish extraordinary things. You don't have to listen to the people around you who question your ability or will to do something great. Learn to surround yourself with people who believe in you and be that person to someone else. Whatever you decide to do, I hope you love people well and open yourself to living life in a fulfilling and memorable way. It's time to write your own adventure.

Now, get after it.

Butcher Paper

Keep writing on the wall, even if they tear it down.

There were three options presented to me when I graduated high school: go to college, get a job, or join the military. The options were explained the same way a car salesman points to color choices to convince a buyer one color has a better resale value than the other. In my school, college was king, but the school's administration applauded all options. The administration's primary concern was to gauge a student's post high school potential and prevent them from making a dumb decision for how they'd spend their time after graduation.

Our administration must have felt like if they could get all students signed up for one of their options, they could dust their hands off as they checked the last box of making us a "success." Most student's decisions came mostly from parental pressures and the fear of going against the grain, but for some reason, I didn't struggle with either of those forces. My parents didn't try to be overly influential in my decision. In fact, they didn't say a whole lot about what came after high school for me. I didn't see creativity, adventure, or whimsy in any of the predetermined options, and I felt I'd be settling if I committed to one of the prescribed paths.

My high school was large, and most of its students came from middle-class households. My graduating class saw 417 students walk across the stage to receive their diploma. Of those hundreds of students, there were at least a few I didn't recognize. I think they were imposters.

The school was public, but it was certainly a few notches up from public schools in other parts of Alabama. We had outstanding teachers, and generally, great kids. Typical high school problems were present at my school, just like anybody else's. Kids occasionally got busted at a party, there was the occasional fight, and we always had more ambition than talent on our football team. I was fortunate to have graduated from the high school I attended.

My school's administration championed the idea college would be the best option for most students, and truthfully, for most, it was. Most kids at my school had the ability to go to college, at least at a state school. Parents and teachers held academics with high regard. There was little excuse not to achieve what was necessary to be accepted to a higher education institution.

Our teachers seemed to genuinely care for their students, and they poured more than required into us. Most kids were able to obtain a scholarship, or their family had the money to support them throughout college. The only kids who chose a path other than college did so deliberately, just like I did. We were all very fortunate to have choices in front of us, and it's something I appreciate more today than I did at the time.

Like many high schools, senior year served as the final stretch in preparing students for college. We did all the routine college application procedures. Kids took the ACT or SAT, made a list of desired colleges, and always included at least one "reach" school. It was clear, even to the casual observer, college was the preferred choice for my school's administration and my classmates' parents. At the end of it all, most everyone awaited eagerly for a "yes" or "no" from the schools they had applied to.

As my senior year ended, my school hung a giant piece of butcher paper on the science hall. Teachers instructed students to write their name and their plans for after graduation. My school did this to encourage kids to share what was in their future, but the butcher paper was also a self-serving pat on the administration's back. Regardless of the administration's intentions, the kids approached the butcher paper with excitement.

Most students scribbled which college they had committed to, and a few simply wrote "military." It was apparent how prestigious a university someone was accepted to by how big they inscribed the wall. I fell into this category, but only because I knew my contribution would cause a ruffle. By the end of my senior year, I had committed myself to packing my bags and heading to a tiny village in eastern Ukraine, not far from the Russian border.

Although it goes against my introverted tendencies, I've never been opposed to people disagreeing with me, so I decided to cause a stir. I knew deep down I'd never follow through with my crazy idea if I didn't go for it right out of high school. There's nothing anyone could have said to me to change my mind. I'm stubborn like that.

In big, bold letters, I printed my name and, and in even bigger font, simply wrote "Ukraine." Half the people in my school couldn't tell you where Ukraine was, and to be honest, I couldn't have either a year prior. I didn't understand the immediate draw to college right out of high school, and I wanted to consider life outside the prescribed borders. From my perspective, colleges would still be there whenever I was ready for them. Sure, I'd miss out on a few experiences with my friends who were going to college, but I figured sacrificing time with them would be worth it if I had a big enough idea to latch onto.

Many people thought I was crazy and questioned why I would want to move to a foreign country instead of beginning college with my closest friends. It was simple in my mind. I knew college would be there when I got home, so I figured I didn't have much to lose. Throwing caution to the wind wasn't something I was known for, but I understood I had the opportunity to do something interesting and exciting, so I decided to go all-in. I mean, what could go wrong?

The summer before my senior year, my church's youth group took a trip to Kiev, Ukraine to show God's love to orphaned kids. We didn't explain it to the government like that; instead, we told them we were there to "help the kids with English." The Gospel isn't illegal in Ukraine, but we figured we'd have fewer eyes looking at us from the government if we just left the "Christian" title out of it. Having successfully duped everyone into letting us have two weeks with the kids at camp, we set off to teach the truths of the Bible. We had one or two classes about basic English grammar and vocabulary, but mostly our Ukrainian translators helped us talk to these kids about Jesus.

Before this trip, I had never left America but thought it would be a fulfilling experience while working towards a worthy cause. All of my best friends were going on the trip too, so I figured at the very least, we'd have a great time and make lasting memories. Our goal was simple: help a few locals in Kiev run a Christian summer camp for Ukrainian orphans and pray to see their hearts changed.

The camp wasn't anything magical or extravagant, it was just a typical summer camp. Lots of kids ran around screaming, people didn't bathe much, the food was terrible, and everyone had a great time. God used the camp to bring many kids to know

Him, but He also used it as a seed in my heart, which sprouted into a major life change.

It didn't dawn on me at the time, but God used my first trip out of the United States to grab my attention and affection for Ukraine and its people. After thinking and praying through such a significant life change, I couldn't escape the desire to go back to Ukraine. My mind and heart became consumed by the idea of returning. I didn't exactly know what I would be doing or who I would live with, I simply knew I wanted to go.

My vision became laser-focused on Ukraine. It's a bit alarming how unprepared I was in terms of a plan, but I guess that's how it goes when you're seventeen. All I saw in front of me was a grand adventure and the hopes of helping little kids in Ukraine, which was enough for me to say, "I'm in."

By the end of my senior year of high school, I had already applied for a visa, sent out fundraising letters, and maybe most bold of all, told others of my plan. The truth is, I didn't have an intricate plan. Blame it on my young mind, or just sheer recklessness, but I didn't care about the fine details. I just wanted to go. I wanted to do something special and meaningful.

I wrestled with the possibility of my decision potentially being a massive mistake. After all, my closest friends were making plans to room together at the University of Alabama, and I knew I wouldn't be anywhere near them for quite a while after graduation. I remember praying for God to speak to me, just to give me a sign I was making the right decision. I sometimes looked to the sky, hoping God had used an airplane to write a message to me. That never happened, but I knew He would walk beside me throughout my journey.

I couldn't help wondering if my decision to move across the globe was a wise one. I struggled with the idea of my friends forgetting about me or the possibility of altogether missing God's calling in my life. By the end of my senior year, those questions grew louder in my head, but I was already locked in. Writing my plan on the butcher paper in my high school was the final declaration to those watching. I was going to Ukraine.

Despite my fear of the decision I'd made, I proudly walked by my public proclamation between classes. Each pass reminded me of the excitement and adventure which awaited me. I'd often give not-so-subtle glances towards my post if I thought there was any chance a passing classmate would follow my eyes to the wall. I looked forward to seeing the wall each time the bell rang until one day I noticed someone had scribbled my addition out.

At first, I thought it was a prank by some of my friends, so I happily rewrote my plans next to my original post. I was a little excited to redo my post as I thought it was just another chance for someone to catch me writing "Ukraine" by my name on the wall. Maybe this time someone would stop to ask me what I meant or where Ukraine was. It was a self-aggrandizing approach, but it kept me from allowing doubt to creep in.

I wanted to talk about my plans. I was secretly hoping someone would confront me about them. My desire for attention stemmed from a mixture of pride and the need for encouragement. Pride is the ugly side of the equation; it's the part I have continually tried to banish from my life as I've gotten older. Encouragement, on the other hand, is something we all strive for, something we all need.

As my senior year of high school ended, I found a strange sense of encouragement through the doubts and whispers I overheard from my classmates. I couldn't blame them, I was the one with the crazy plans, and even I didn't understand everything. I couldn't expect them to grasp my sense of adventure. Moving to a foreign country was unconventional, and the background noise of my life was a constant reminder of that.

Not long after someone had etched my words out the first

time, it became clear there was a repeat offender. "No problem," I thought, "Just one more chance for me to make my post even bigger and closer to the kid who wrote 'Harvard' next to their name." Who was that Harvard guy anyway? He was praised for following his dreams and achievements. Why couldn't I get a little love for what I was doing?

After I loosened my grip on the grudge I was holding, I wrote "Ukraine" on the butcher paper once more, and all was well as I walked away with a smile and confidence. The day soon came when not only were my words etched out, they were completely missing. Somebody had taken a pair of scissors and cut my post from the wall. It was completely gone. I was less joyful when I noticed the absence of my intriguing plans this time around, especially when I learned my school's administration was behind the foul play.

The thing is, my school's administration didn't believe me. Or maybe they didn't believe *in* me. They thought I was making a bad joke by writing some post-Soviet country on the wall instead of a state school. They couldn't conceive any reason why someone from their school, with all the privileges bestowed upon their students, would want to forgo college in pursuit of a crazy idea. Looking back, I see why they may have felt the way they did, but I couldn't see it at the time.

The school's actions made me angry and, truthfully, a little discouraged. They were the adults who were supposed to have all the answers, and now they seemed to be in overt opposition to me. I was confused and slightly embarrassed that I had been unsuccessful in obtaining their support.

I'll likely never know the underlying reasons the members of my high school's administration forcefully redacted my plans from their walls. I now understand some people feel threatened or jealous when someone has something they don't. Maybe whoever cut my writing off the wall wished they had a more exciting life, or perhaps they had dreams they never achieved. I've learned most people don't like when someone around them has big ideas or plans. It makes them feel insecure to see someone attempting something out of the norm. Unfortunately, that outlook sometimes makes them discouraging or even downright mean to others when they don't understand what others are doing or why they're doing it.

Ambition is threatening, and action taunts lazy or uninspired people. I've certainly been guilty of holding these negative views against self-progression towards people in my own life, and it's an ugly part of my history. We do this to ourselves sometimes too. We question our plans and ideas because we don't have anyone in our lives we can look to for a model of how to get from point A to point B. It's a logical thing. We want familiarity, security, and comfort. But, it's also a dangerous mindset.

Humans are taught to avoid danger and risk. But, what happens when we decide to throw those things to the wind, even for just a brief time, just to see what we are capable of? What if we all decided to muster the courage to be bold in our desires to see what journey they take us on? What if God has plans for our lives that require more than the status quo and more leaning on Him to make something extraordinary happen?

Our evolutionary instincts and God's plans are sometimes at odds with each other. These differences aren't a mistake. It's more plausible God intentionally allows us to put our heads and our hearts in opposition at times. Leaving the fears and reservations that echo in my head to follow my heart often results in stories that point back to Jesus, so that's where I placed my hope as I graduated high school.

As I made my plans known my senior year, I learned something interesting happens when you choose not to follow life's ordinary course. All at once, there seems to be nothing that can stop you, not even those you call "ma'am" or "sir." Things that once seemed important drift away until they are unrecognizable. When we turn our attention towards eternity, our legacy, and a life filled with purpose, we begin to replace things in our lives that have a shelf life with things determined to stand the test of time.

Life is made of choices and consequences, and I didn't want my high school's administration to be the one choosing those things for me. The goals they envisioned seemed more secure, but I also knew I'd be just another number to them as I finally walked across the graduation stage. It seemed silly to agree to their terms when I knew life had more to offer than they were telling me about. I appreciated their offer of a sure path, but I didn't want it.

I am no different than you. If we're honest with ourselves, we all want things that are unconventional or beyond the current perimeters of our lives. Some of us want a different job, a wild adventure, better relationships, or just the feeling of being alive again. Many of us have lost the imagination we had as a kid, and we've filled the void with fear and doubt. Don't get me wrong; some fear and doubt is a healthy thing. I don't suggest you quit your job and join a band if you can't play an instrument or sing. Certain restrictions in life are healthy, but choosing to live a safe life instead of a fulfilling one is not.

There's something threatening to some when you express your grand ideas to others. God has made us all different, and not all of us want to live on the edge of our seats. Some of you will thrive in this "against the grain" move, but others will continually allow doubt to creep in if you're not careful. Be wise in your plans, but also be bold. Know what you want to do, then make a plan to accomplish your goal.

As you look forward to whatever your plan is, remember a few things. There will be those who think you're crazy, others will doubt you, and some will simply be mean. We may grow out of our kindergarten bodies, but I assure you, some people live their entire lives with the same mean-hearted and nasty attitudes we all battled on the playground of our youth. You have the ability, and the choice, to view those people with love and kindness. It may take someone like you to be the voice of love and patience in their lives to show them they too have what it takes to create a meaningful and worthwhile life filled with whimsy and purpose.

Whatever you choose to do, I promise you a "normal" life will be waiting for you if you ever want to return. My hope is you will find something so meaningful and worthwhile that it seems crazy to go back. I also hope you'll learn to encourage others to do the same. On your journey ahead, you will be forced to examine yourself on a deeper level, and there will be days you question why you ever believed in the dream you're after. On those days, know that fear exits through the same door hope knocks on.

You won't do everything correctly, and you'll likely need someone to extend a helping hand along the way. You'll have people who may want to tear your ideas off the wall, but you'll also have people who love and support you. Nobody can accomplish your dreams for you, but it's alright to ask for help. Be someone's help, and allow them to be yours. You will both be better off because of it.

Can I Live with You?
Ask the question that could change your life.

Like many high school kids, I never lived outside of my parents' house before graduating, and I didn't have a clue how to do a lot of the things adults do. The idea of finding a place to live outside of my parents' place was something I had never considered, much less finding a home in a foreign country. At the time, most of my friends were making arrangements to live in college dorms, so my peer support level was pretty low considering they knew as much as I did about the process I was navigating. My parents are great people, but they didn't choose to pursue a path similar to mine, so they too lacked in the practical advice department. They provided support and encouragement but were a little less helpful in the "here's what you need to do" conversations. Just like anything else in life, I learned as I went, but I'm certainly not blind to the fact God was guiding me the entire way.

Luckily, I knew a family in my town who was well-versed in world travel and had an international network. The father of the family owned his own business, and it had done well. They were fortunate in their ability to be afforded more financial freedom and time together than most other families I knew.

This family had similar affections for Ukraine and its people as I did. In fact, they already had a few kids who they had adopted from Ukraine years ago.

I was good friends with this family's oldest son and saw his house as my second home. Their house seemed more similar to a never-ending summer camp than it did someone's private residence. There seemed always to be more people running around their property than they may have wished at times. Anyone remotely close to this family knew of their open-door policy and regularly took advantage of it. I'm not sure even they had a key to their house because I never once noticed the doors locked.

At one point, this family had a half-pipe in their back yard for skateboarding. They got wind a few of us were into skateboarding and took it upon themselves to give us the best shot at becoming the next Tony Hawk. After a few broken bones and close brushes with their homeowner's insurance, they took it down and replaced the area with a small basketball court. It was a wise move.

With all of the kids and teenagers constantly running around their house, practical jokes seemed to be never-ending. Once when this family was away on a trip, my friends and I decided to play a prank on them and found a way to park a full-size sedan in their living room to watch TV from. A few online news channels highlighted our escapade, which, in turn, was our downfall. We found the boundaries with that joke, but we all made up afterward.

This family lived life the way I intended to. They didn't adhere to the way life was "supposed" to be done. They seemed to view every opportunity as a window into a grand adventure and didn't care they were different than most other families.

I wondered for a few weeks if this family could help me navigate my international move, but I struggled to find the courage to ask them for help. I knew if I let on to my crazy idea, they would probably never let me hear the end of it, and I'd have to move to Ukraine for the rest of my life. This family was serious about approaching life in a way that poured into people, and they weren't ones to dismiss outlandish ideas. I eventually decided a conversation with them was in my best interest, so I reached out to see if they could give me advice.

My conversation with them was similar to the awkward conversations you might have with a new girlfriend or boyfriend during high school. I fumbled my way through explaining the adventure I was considering, but I was careful not to make eye contact too often. I feared eye contact would make me feel more awkward, so I allowed my eyes to bounce around the room instead. After explaining my plan to move to Ukraine, they acted like I told them I was considering going to the movies that night. There weren't any raised eyebrows. They told me it was a funny coincidence, but they knew an American family who lived in eastern Ukraine who just happened to be in the States the following week. They said they'd be having dinner with them and invited me along. I accepted, but not without a head-spinning amount of confusion and feeling of luck.

As we all sat down to dinner a week later, I was introduced to a man named Adam and his wife, Charlotte. Adam is a man from rural Louisiana, and his thick Southern accent doesn't leave any question to the fact. His wife is a sweet lady who cares for those around her. Adam and Charlotte are both simple people who seem to find joy in the most mundane things in life, and both certainly have big hearts. Adam also doesn't mind picking a little fun at your expense, but he doesn't mean anything by it. It's just how he is.

I was nervous and excited, both in equal parts, because I knew the question I was about to ask Adam had the potential to radically change my life. I didn't have a presentation prepared to explain why I wanted to move half way across the world, instead, I had an ambition to tell them about. The only thing I could offer was the promise to dream big and to be open to the unknown. My only hope was Adam and Charlotte would be receptive to my aspiration and see a bit of their younger selves in me.

When we sat down at dinner, we entertained several minutes of awkward chat. Even with the imposing question we both knew I would eventually ask, I had decided to exchange common pleasantries before diving into the serious stuff. The family who set our meal up had primed Adam and his wife for the question I'd be asking them, and I think that fueled Adam's mischievous tendencies.

Adam would have let me talk for hours without making the slightest move towards to real reason we were talking. He allowed me to wander into the meaningless area of chat, which reveals only how someone feels about the weather or some distant sports team they vaguely follow. Adam enjoyed watching me squirm my way through the conversation while he tested the pressure points of social norms. That's just kind of the guy he is. He likes to laugh and have a good time, and he knew I'd be dropping a big question as soon as I got the courage. Until then, Adam was enjoying the show.

Finally, I blurted out, "Can I live with you?" Adam was talking, and I cut him off. I didn't mean to, but my words exited my mouth without my instruction. It was a little anti-climactic as the question hung in the air. I was expecting a few questions and the "let me think about it" routine where I would have to endlessly replay the conversation in my head to look for subtle clues as to what the determination would ultimately be.

There was no such thing. Adam didn't have even the slightest concern or reservation. He simply told me to pack my bags and meet him and his family in Ukraine when I was ready. It was almost as if I asked him if I could stay the night at his house while passing through town, only I'd be staying much longer.

On the one hand, it was relieving to hear such a simple response. Still, on the other, I internally panicked as I realized our conversation had sealed the deal. I didn't know where exactly Adam lived in Ukraine, I wasn't sure of the date I'd move, and I certainly didn't know what life would be like, but at least I had a place to stay. Too many people knew my plans at this point, and I wasn't going to back out. I didn't realize it at the time, but those five simple words I asked Adam provided the first sketches of a roadmap for my future in Ukraine.

After leaving dinner, I went directly home to tell my parents the news. I first had to find Lugansk on a map to verify it was actually in Ukraine, but soon after confirmation, I was in full motion. Before I knew it, I was excitedly looking up one-way plane tickets to Lugansk, Ukraine. It's funny looking back because I didn't even know how to say "Lugansk" correctly, and there I was looking for a one-way ticket.

In all my excitement, I almost forgot I didn't have any money, and I hadn't been approved by the Ukrainian government to live in their country. It didn't matter much to me at the time that I would have to seek a foreign government's approval to fulfill my dream of moving to Ukraine. I just figured they'd be happy to have me.

As I settled back into reality, I figured I should probably get to work on answering a couple of questions before moving forward. My plan of action quickly became writing a letter and sending it to every person I knew. If I would have had your address, I would likely have sent a letter to your mailbox as well. I wanted my letter to express the whimsy and excitement I had in mind when I thought of moving to a foreign country, but I also wanted it to be honest and straightforward with the fact I needed money. My goal was to meet orphaned

Ukrainian kids and show them Jesus, but I needed help getting there.

I'm a bit of a romantic when it comes to writing letters. I have to be honest in telling you I ended up scrapping a few drafts that promised to end world hunger and disease. After many iterations, my letter was complete, and I taped it to the wall as I stood back to admire its beauty and genius. After I came back to my senses, I stuffed as many envelopes as I could with my message. I sensed amounts of excitement and nervousness similar to an engaged couple sending wedding invitations announcing to the world their intentions to join themselves before all. For better or worse, my intentions were soon to stand in front of everyone I knew.

Soon after my tongue recovered from licking stacks of envelopes, the "what ifs" started to creep in. I became filled with doubt as I second-guessed myself and my abilities. Who was I to believe I could move to a foreign country to show love to orphaned children? I began to fear my plans were arrogant and foolish, but I also knew fear would show itself in various forms throughout my journey.

Following a considerable amount of waiting and second-guessing myself, I began receiving replies to my letter. Many responses were filled with well-wishes and promises to pray, but even fewer included financial support. Now, as an adult writing this book, I realize better what I was asking other people. I wanted them to provide their money, something they worked hard for and needed for their families, to take a chance on me in my outlandish endeavor. I get a little embarrassed looking back at my request. I'm sure, to some, my plans seemed dumb or even reckless.

Each letter addressed to me that arrived in my parents' mailbox felt like gold in my hands. I paused each time the mailman delivered a response to my crazy idea, and I treated each envelope with respect and off-the-chart levels of anticipation. Before opening each response, my mind raced between extreme hope and utter disappointment for what was inside. I began to question God's voice and calling and even thought I had been foolish for thinking of such a crazy idea. I mean, seriously, what kid moves across the ocean to a foreign country on his own? The confidence I had in myself and in my plan dwindled as I began to consider the possibility of my efforts being ultimately futile and even laughable. I think God knew this and provided a renewed sense of excitement and "what if" each time I went to my parents' mailbox.

Regardless of how I felt about things at the time, God knew what I needed, and He provided. When I counted up all of the responses, people had donated over $13,000 to me. I was blown away by peoples' generosity but was also well aware the point of turning back had passed me.

Soon after I received enough money for a one-way plane ticket, I bought the cheapest airline ticket I could find and stuffed the remaining cash in a shoebox to take with me. Now with a one-way plane ticket in hand, my departure date raced closer and closer on the horizon. One thing was for sure, two weeks after graduating high school, I was to be wheels up headed across the Atlantic Ocean.

I continued to engage with my friends who were making plans for who they'd room with their freshman year at college, which provided brief moments of second-guessing my future. Regardless of my occasional self-doubt, a few guys organized a send-off party the night before I left for Ukraine. I didn't know how long I'd be in Ukraine, so I decided to treat our gathering as a farewell of sorts. We all stayed up the entire night, sitting in my room, sharing stories that dated almost a decade before. We laughed, prayed, and reminisced about times past and anticipated memories to come.

At one point, we even decided to go in the front yard and box each other with big, green, Hulk gloves. The cops rolled by, but it seemed they enjoyed the entertainment and left us alone. We were just a bunch of kids who were excited about each of our futures, and we simply desired to spend time together.

Just before sunrise, I decided it would be wise to pack a bag to take with me to Ukraine. I found my mom's old floral suitcase, probably from the 1980s, and filled it the same as I would if I were going on a family vacation. I figured whatever I forgot wasn't too important, or I would have remembered to pack it.

As the sun broke the horizon, my parents came to my room and informed me it was time to go to the airport. I tossed my suitcase and skateboard into the trunk and settled into the driver seat of my car as my parents took the passenger seats. My friends piled into their vehicles, and we set off towards the Birmingham airport. After we arrived, we all sat in the airport's lobby, just shy of the security checkpoint, and shared our last goodbyes.

To my surprise, a few more friends showed up to encourage me in what I was about to take on. My mom sat quietly in the corner, observing all that was happening as a few silent tears rolled down her face. She was proud of me but also worried. The morning I left brought about a rollercoaster of emotions for me, but especially for my mom. She has a big heart and was going to miss her son.

We all stretched the minutes to my boarding as long as possible. Laughter, hugs, and well-wishes filled each passing moment. The time finally came when I hugged each person for the last time and walked towards my gate. I felt equal amounts of support, love, and fear as I rolled on my skateboard around the first corner, obscuring my view of the people I love most. As a long-haired kid fresh out of high school, the uncertainty of what life was about to be like started to set in as I walked down the jet bridge and onto the plane.

Reality was setting in, and my stomach was in knots of excitement and doubt. I didn't know it at the time, but God was about to start my journey to Ukraine with a bang. Soon, I'd be the kid in the deep end of the pool with only floaties around my arms and not enough rhythm to tread water on my own. God wasn't going to let me drown, but there would be plenty of arm flailing and panic to come.

As my time in Ukraine taught me over and over, I continue to be amazed at how God works things out when I am acting upon His plans. God doesn't require us to know every step of the plan for action to be initiated. Sometimes life is as simple as saying, "I'll go," even if the destination or directions are unclear. God delights in our childlike approach in trusting Him. The Lord talks about how He sustains the birds of the air and the flowers of the fields and commands us to trust Him. Jesus calls us not to worry, but to have faith in Him.

If you're like me, it's often hard to know what God's plans are, and you have a habit of injecting your ideas of what should happen into the plan. We all do it, and I don't think it's anything to be ashamed of. Adam and Eve did it, and we are sinners just like them.

I'm certainly no expert at distinguishing God's will from my own; in fact, my batting average has to be pretty low. God's plans often make my head tilt on axis with an inquisitive murmur of "Are you sure about that?" Yet, this is one of the things that make following Christ so interesting and fulfilling. I've made plenty of mistakes and have been humbled many times as a result when I think I'm reaching towards God's plan for my life, but God continues to be faithful.

There have been times when I thought I sensed God pushing me towards specific journeys or ideas, and I ended up figuring out it was just my plan all along. It happens. Other times, like finding a home in Ukraine, it seemed almost too easy, like I was missing something or what I was doing was a trap. God intentionally places setbacks and allows serious doubt when we are chasing after Him. Each time I've been met with those things in my walk with Christ, I am reminded of His goodness and faithfulness, even in the times I am so shortsighted I can't even see my own hand in front of my face. One thing I have learned is God will never leave me hanging. His hand is always outstretched. Most of the time, I simply have to stop second-guessing myself long enough to reach out and grab it.

With these ideas bouncing around my head, I was barreling towards Ukraine as the wheels retracted into the plane. God was seated next to me. As I stared out of the window, I began to realize the God of the Universe made the earth beneath me and the sky I now soared across. That same God was also thinking of me. I wasn't on the plane by mistake, God had paved the way for me. He knew my fears, my doubts, and my excitement and looked towards me and said, "Let's do this together."

Fountain Pen
Live a life worth remembering.

I had a neighbor named Jay growing up. He was retired and spent most of his days in his garage tinkering with whatever suited his interest for the day. Jay was the type of guy who always had a story and didn't seem to pick up on any social cues that I had somewhere else to be or something else to do. In his world, it was him and whoever was in front of him. Nothing else mattered.

Jay was in his sixties when I lived next door to him, but you wouldn't be able to tell by looking at him. I often ran into him at the YMCA, where he led a fitness class as I was in the corner grunting, doing my own workout. It seemed Jay never stopped moving. He had an itch to improve himself and engage with those around him continually. He was also the kind of guy who always seemed genuinely interested in the lives around him and wanted to hear what others had to say. I admired this about Jay because his attitude was infectious and encouraging.

My parents' driveway ran parallel with Jay's. Only a small patch of grass separated the two. In fact, I used to jump over the divide on my skateboard as a kid. Don't be fooled into thinking I was good at skateboarding. I wasn't. If I had given you a skate-board, you too could have jumped the small patch of grass.

Jay seemed always to be outside or just beyond the threshold of his open garage door, ready to engage anyone who walked by. I'm pretty sure he had one of those mounted binocu-lars you slip a quarter into often found at the top of a mountain. There was nothing to hide Jay's sight-line to my parents' house, so I had to remain vigilant as I came and went. If I wasn't care-ful, he'd spot me from a distance and have me in his conversa-tional crosshairs.

I used to scout the premises for any sign of Jay whenever I needed to leave home and was in a hurry to get somewhere. I didn't mind speaking with Jay, but I knew my schedule was at his mercy and often not compatible with his. I would peek out of the window, which overlooked where I parked my car, to see if the path was clear. If I was extra careful, I'd sneak out of my parents' front door and peer over the bushes as I tried to blend in with them.

Somehow, I often missed the signs of Jay's presence and found myself roped into a conversation, which typically lasted anywhere from twenty minutes to three hours. I'm reasonably sure he knew a rough outline of my daily schedule and would hide in the corner of his basement then pop out at the last moment. He kept me on my toes as I walked to my car each day. It almost seemed like a game.

In cases of desperation, I'd use the age-old fake phone conversation as I approached my car. I didn't like doing this because deep down, I enjoyed talking to Jay, and I felt I owed him some of my time. Plus, I got caught once by Jay as I was "talking" on my phone when it rang.

Jay always seemed to have a challenge in his conversations with me. Sometimes our conversations were politically moti-vated, other times spiritually. Most of the time, Jay wanted me to consider different possibilities and approaches to the things he was thinking through. I don't think he ever needed input from me, but he always seemed to want it. It certainly wasn't anything I offered that made him want to talk, but he had a deep-rooted desire for conversation with anyone who would take the time.

One day, Jay caught me coming home and went in for the kill. I could see it coming before I pulled into the driveway, and I knew I was in for a long conversation. I considered driving away and coming back later in the cover of night, but it was too late. Jay had spotted me.

As I exited my car, he quickly walked across the thin grass median and was ready to talk before both of my feet hit the earth. Truthfully, I didn't want to talk, but I couldn't escape Jay. I was tired from a day at school, and I had things to get done around the house. It didn't matter though, he had been on a sniping mission, and I was now in the center of his scope.

As I reluctantly exited my car, Jay was mid-way through his first thought. I don't remember what about, but he was in the groove. Jay was locked on a topic he found interesting, and he wanted me to know all about it. I nodded along as I usually did, interjecting words which didn't take more than two syllables. Then, out of nowhere, Jay invited me to do something he'd never asked before. He wanted me to come into his basement to look at something he had been working on.

I thought his request was strange. Even though his house was not more than twenty feet from our fireside chats, he never invited me inside. Entering an elderly man's kingdom, the workshop in his basement, was unthinkable. I was instantly engaged and on full alert. The workshop in his basement seemed too sacred of a place. Jay guarded it more than an old man stands watch over his lawn. Regardless of my confusion, I accepted the invitation and followed him inside his sacred ground.

As we crossed the threshold, we eased past mounted animal heads from his hunting trips out west and eventually found ourselves standing at his workbench. The workbench itself was meticulously organized and clean. Tools hung neatly above the dark-stained wooden work surface. Despite what he was about to reveal to me, there wasn't a speck of dust anywhere.

After a short presentation worthy of an Oscar acceptance speech, Jay handed me a felt-lined box and a leather-bound journal. Little did I know he had been practicing making bespoke wooden fountain pens entirely from scratch, which is exactly what was in the felt-lined box. I was equally confused and amazed by what was in front of me, but I knew Jay had a reason behind his gift.

The pen was made from real wood and had a glossy finish, which clarified the grain. It had gold accents and an engraved logo Jay had designed. The pen was of high quality and certainly worth a fair amount of money. The journal was fashioned from genuine tan leather and had a magnetic latch which secured it shut. The pages inside were thick and high quality, but empty and ready to be ink-soaked and transformed into something meaningful.

I was instantly stunned. It was apparent Jay had spent a lot of time designing and perfecting the gifts now in front of me. Jay enjoyed sharing his craft with me, and he took careful notice of the way I stared in amazement and confusion towards what he had just handed me. I thought it was strange he was giving me a gift, but he knew I was moving to Ukraine, so I figured he was trying to encourage me.

Jay noticed my puzzled face as he clarified the reason for his gift. He told me I should use the pen and journal to record my experiences in Ukraine. He tasked me with writing about the people I met, the things I did, what I felt, and to keep them forever as a reminder of the journey I was about to embark on. I have to admit, as a seventeen-year-old guy, I thought the idea of journaling was an odd thing, but I decided to take Jay's advice while I was abroad to see what happened. Someone like Jay had clearly lived a full life with the number of stories and anecdotes he stood ready to provide at any given time, so I figured he must be onto something with this journaling idea.

During my time in Ukraine, it was rare for me to go a day without writing in the journal Jay had gifted me. The pen and journal went everywhere I did and became a constant in my life. Writing became a refuge for me and a friend who helped navigate my thoughts and feelings. Sometimes my thoughts were concise and pointed. Other times my hand remained in constant motion as my brain attempted to untangle my emotions.

My journal's pages chronicled my daily activities, prayers, and the multitude of emotions that bounced around my head and heart. The pages never questioned my motives and always left me feeling more encouraged than when I opened it. Pen and paper became my therapist while I was living overseas. Without Jay and his gifts to me, I don't believe this book would have come to life.

Ten years had passed since I returned to America when I gained the courage to open the densely inscribed pages of the journal Jay had given me. I originally planned to read my words on the long journey back to the States, but I couldn't pull myself to do it when the time came. With hundreds of pages filled, I had forgotten what many of them said. As I soared between two worlds, I wasn't ready to unpack the last nine months of my adventure just yet.

When the time finally came to examine the words I had written, I sat night after night, carefully reading each entry. I typed each word from my journal onto my computer to reconnect with what I was experiencing when I first wrote the words. Each keystroke mimicked the dragging and pushing of the pen I had committed to so many years before. The process was therapeutic and often exposed raw emotion from memories that had escaped my mind.

As I reconnected with my memories, I began to realize the kindness and forethought Jay had for me all those years ago. My neighbor, the man I often ducked from, had spent a part of his life thinking of me and used his talents to craft a gift that would give life and joy to me years after he presented it to me. I began to feel sad and embarrassed for all the times I tried to escape Jay. He put me before himself in those times, but I couldn't see it at my young age.

I can't help but see God when thinking of Jay's gift. It's evident how God used Jay to push me towards recording such a critical time in my life, knowing how impactful it would be to me later. I'm not sure if Jay realized it or not, but his act of kindness and thoughtfulness resonated with me in a way that has set my sights upon doing the same for others. "What can I do for someone that will matter in ten years" is now in my vocabulary.

Jay died unexpectedly a few years ago. He wasn't a particularly old man in the grand scheme of things, but his days were numbered just like mine and yours. Until his last day, Jay lived his life to the fullest. My parents have moved houses, and my wife and I have moved all around the country over the past decade, but I now have a ritual whenever I find myself near Jay's house. When I can, I drive by his old home and reminisce about the times I avoided him in our practically shared driveways. While I balance the delicate task of driving slowly enough by his old house to let memories flood my mind but quickly enough not to get the cops called, I think back to the times he would talk, and I would listen. Like many people I've heard say before, I wish I could have one more conversation with Jay just to let him know he meant something to me.

It's obvious to me now how a life well-lived, like Jay's, full of questions and a curious outlook, is well worth the time and effort spent. His life encourages me to slow down and consider life's questions. I think many of us, including myself, get into a rut of smoothing out life's edges until we've extracted the whimsy and adventure from it. Jay seemed to have welcomed the peaks and valleys and took delight in knowing he didn't understand everything. This sort of outlook seemed to keep him engaged and interested in life.

I'll likely never know if Jay included me in his wondering moments of questioning more for my benefit or his. I'll also never know if he kept any record of the conversations we shared. I guess I'll never be sure Jay ever even thought much about the conversations we shared, but I know they have helped shape the man I am today. I'm thankful to him for that.

At the core of it, I believe we all have a Jay in our lives. If we spent the time to look back at people in our paths, we'd all see someone who went out of their way in an attempt to apply their legacy to our timeline. For some people, it's our parents or grandparents; for others, it's a teacher or a friend. Heck, for some, it's the police or a strict school principal. No matter the case, that one person we think of had our best interests in mind when they acted in our lives.

The question I often ask myself these days is how I become that person for someone else. If you're like me, you fall into the trap of believing you don't have anything to offer others. Perhaps you tell yourself you're too young or too average to believe you have valuable input. Even worse, you may live in a culture that devalues your voice. No matter your case, you have something to offer others.

Your life bears importance, meaning, and a unique outlook, which is precisely what someone else is looking to learn from. Don't allow the world around you, your school or office, your home or friends, or even your self-perception trick you into believing you can't have an impact on others like Jay had on me. You can bring a positive change to those around you, but you first have to believe in yourself. Jesus calls us to love those around us, and it's something Jay did well.

You and I both have specific talents and abilities gifted to us by God to glorify Him and encourage others. You may be exceptionally smart or an incredibly hard worker. Maybe you're funny or compassionate or a good listener. Others may be financially gifted, and some of you may be a little short on cash but still look at the world, and others, as opportunities to spread joy and love. Truthfully, I don't know my abilities and talents just yet, and you might not know yours either. That's alright. Life is full of self-exploration and discovery, and that shouldn't stop you from using what you have and understand today to positively impact those around you.

As you begin to examine that "thing" you've been wanting to do, start by asking yourself what you want your legacy to be. Who do you want to influence, and for what reason? Don't get trapped in the mindset of your legacy has to mean your name becomes a household one. Your legacy could be so quiet, yet so meaningful, that you affect only one person for the better.

If you're like me, you will struggle with the idea of what you're doing isn't big enough. Don't let that lie find root in your heart. Learn to be so focused and intentional with those around you that whether it be one person beside you in an elevator or 10,000 people in front of you in an auditorium, you leave a lasting impact on your audience. As you decide what it is you will go after – what will become your life's mission – go after it with vigor and don't look back. You have what it takes; you just have to take steps towards believing in yourself.

Learn to take yourself out of the picture. Jesus often looks to the humble and meek to accomplish great things. I believe in you, and you should believe in yourself too. God has a unique plan for your life. Read that again. God has a unique plan for your life, which means the God of the Universe has thought about *you*. How crazy is that? In the times you doubt yourself or you feel unworthy of the task at hand, remember God has placed you there for a reason.

Be encouraged by the fact God thinks about you and adores you. There isn't a day that goes by when Jesus doesn't remember you. The Lord made you with a specific purpose in mind, and He sustains your every breath on earth. On the days you feel down, forgotten about, discouraged, or confused, remember God has allowed you another day to pursue your goal.

You're in the situation you're in now for a reason. You carry the struggles you currently have for a purpose. My challenge for you is to use what God has given you today to pour into the lives of those around you. Just like Jay did, your actions today may live well beyond your intentions and provide life for someone else for years to come. You may end up changing a life.

Vodka and Hairdressers

God listens to our prayers, even if they are simply "Please God, please God, please God."

I thought God would ease me into my new life in Ukraine. After all, I was only seventeen years old, and I had never lived outside of my parents' house. Moving halfway across the world had me scared out of my mind, but excitement masked my fear. I imagined the time it took me to travel to Ukraine would be similar to the start of a race. I wasn't yet running, but I was stepping up to the starting line as I boarded each plane.

Each flight served as a hamstring stretch; I was getting ready for the start gun to go off, but I wasn't prepared to sprint yet. If God was a sports announcer, I imagined He would take the time I was over the Atlantic Ocean to start the "ready, set, go" countdown. Little did I know, He would take the first opportunity to shake things up. By the time the wheels retracted into the plane for my first flight overseas, my confidence had caught a flight headed the opposite direction.

If you've ever been to the Birmingham, Alabama airport, you know you're not flying anywhere without a few layovers. In my case, I had to fly to Chicago before leaving America. A system of tornados winding through the Midwest delayed my flight out of O'Hare for hours, which started a series of missed flights and frustrations. Due to the weather in Chicago, I spent a night sleeping on the airport's cold floor and missed each subsequent connecting flight. Unfortunately, my journey to Ukraine was scheduled to take two days, but it ended up taking four.

By the time I landed in Austria, my first connecting flight outside of the United States, I didn't yet have a cell phone that worked in Europe. The airline companies tossing me around didn't know where I was, but to be fair, I didn't have a clue where I was either. I was only a number to them, and they had hundreds of phone calls identical to the ones from my folks back in America. The airline's best prediction to my parents, and those waiting on me in Ukraine, was I drifted somewhere between Chicago and Lugansk. After several hours of confusion and rerouting, I was ushered to a plane headed east and eventually landed in Kiev, Ukraine.

A friendly guy named Roman was waiting to pick me up in Kiev. I later learned most people referred to him as "curly Roman" because of how his hair spiraled upwards from his head. He had expected me a few days before I arrived and was tired, but he didn't show it. He always seemed to find the good and the funny in every situation. Roman is also an immensely smart and talented individual. He knows English, Ukrainian, Russian, and Chinese, and soon after I arrived in Ukraine, he moved to China to host a Chinese TV show.

He is the kind of person who seemed never to be upset or frustrated. This characteristic proved true the day I first met him. He had been patiently waiting on me for several days in the Kiev airport, holding a sign which simply said "David." Considering Roman didn't know what I looked like, I'm glad nobody else named David was looking for a ride at the airport

that day. I'm pretty sure he would have met him with the same
friendliness and excitement as when we met. Our bodies shared
the same aches and stiff movements after spending sleepless
nights on airport floors, but joining forces in our adventure ener-
gized us.

Despite having never met me before, Roman acted like my
long-lost best friend when he spotted me walking towards him
in the Kiev airport. It was difficult to miss Roman, even from a
distance, because his enthusiasm radiated through his waving
arms and wide smile. His excitement was not my style, as I'm a
rather reserved person socially. But, Roman was the first person
in four days who was excited to see me, so I was pretty amped
up as well. I'm pretty sure God sensed my sigh of relief once I
met up with Roman and hatched a plan to make my adventure a
bit more interesting.

The trip between Kiev and Lugansk required an overnight
train ride, a journey I would become accustomed to during my
time in Ukraine. I learned it was possible to buy tickets to a
small room on the train, which had two sets of bunk beds, a
window, and a table the size of a notebook. Roman, being the
outstanding tour guide he was, had purchased four tickets so we
could have the tiny room for ourselves in an effort to get some
rest on the final leg to Lugansk. Unfortunately, the tickets were
dated for when I was first scheduled to arrive, so my airport
delays made our tickets useless.

Since our tickets were now unusable, we had to purchase
new ones. The only problem was the lady at the ticket counter
in the old Soviet-style train station explained there were only
two tickets left for the entire train. I knew we were in trouble
because I sensed Roman was lobbying for something better than
what she was offering, even though I didn't understand their
conversation. I learned the two remaining tickets were for the

train car lined with people not traveling the full distance across the country, but rather only a few miles to and from work. Those tickets made the Amtrak look like the Taj Mahal. We might have been better off taking our chances hitchhiking across the country instead of buying the remaining tickets.

Roman had a quirk about him. He would sometimes quickly and unintentionally disengage from a conversation as an idea struck him. I have to imagine he has some form of an attention disorder, but rather than a hindrance, it seemed to serve him well. I quickly learned Roman would often turn to whomever he was with and say "pray" as he walked off to accomplish whatever task caught his eye.

My first interaction with Roman's quirk occurred within a few minutes of meeting him. During his conversation with the ticket clerk, he broke his energetic Russian ramble as he quickly turned to me and uttered one English word, "pray," before disappearing. He didn't give a clue to where he was going or any other direction as to what my prayers should be. I decided I'd pray for God simply to help us, but at this point, I didn't know if I should be praying for a train ticket or only for Roman's return.

My prayers worked because a few minutes later, Roman returned and began to smile. I started smiling too, but I still had no idea why. As Roman pushed me along like a parent does to their small children, he finally stopped and turned to me. He explained someone had returned two tickets for a semi-private room, and we would get to buy them. The only catch was we'd have to share our little room with two random people. Sharing the room with two strangers was a far better deal than sitting upright for over eleven hours, so I cheerfully told him it was no problem. Roman seemed a little hush-hush about the whole thing, so I resolved not to make eye contact with anyone and play the dumb foreigner card until we reached our room. After

Roman's negotiating and my "throw a dart and hope it hits" style praying, we were finally ready to board the soon departing train.

Our train car had a narrow hallway on the right side and small private rooms lining the left side. Each room had a sliding wood door with a lock, which a coin could easily defeat. The rooms weren't modern or particularly luxurious, but they offered privacy and a place to sleep while lying flat. A small window allowed natural light to fill each private room, which offered me a chance to study my new environment as the train followed the tracks to Lugansk.

After settling into our glovebox-sized room, Roman and I noticed the remaining two bunks were empty, and the train was already in motion. I heard a sigh of relief from both of us during our premature, yet quiet, rejoicing. We both decided not to acknowledge the two empty bunks in our four-person room. Maybe we wouldn't jinx it if we didn't mention it.

God must have been plotting His next move for a while. Just as Roman and I got comfortable, the sliding door to our room opened with the same violent force of the tornados which had kept me grounded in Chicago just a couple of days before. Four middle-aged Ukrainian ladies towered in the doorway laughing like the Wicked Witch of the West as they stared at their new roommates. They wore brightly colored dresses, and their hair and makeup made them look like they were movie stars. Not "A" list movie stars, but they could pass as an extra in a movie at least.

I'm not sure what was more flamboyant, their attire, or their attitude. The ladies must have spent the immediate time before boarding the train in the train station bar because they reeked of vodka and a healthy dose of perfume. Surely, they had the wrong room, I thought. After all, there were four of them and only two remaining bunks. The ratio of people to beds didn't seem to bother the ladies as they packed in and plumped down on the bunk across from me. The bottle of vodka, which emerged from one of their purses, showed they were ready to continue partying as they now passed the bottle among themselves. The ladies had noticed Roman's curly hair based on their pointing and Roman's blushed face. Roman was either too kind or too embarrassed to let the ladies know his hair was just fine the way it was. It wasn't long, however, until they turned their attention to me. At the time, I had relatively long hair myself, almost shoulder length. My hair wasn't curly, and it certainly didn't have a specific hairstyle; it looked more like a mop on my head. After the ladies discovered two young guys sitting across from them who were obviously in an '80's rock band, they decided to make our heads their petting zoo. They tugged and ruffled our hair, examining it close up and then from far away. I nervously looked to Roman, who returned my anxious glances but offered no relief. Our concerned looks didn't deter the ladies as they began to ramble louder and louder while parting our hair and examining it from all angles.

It soon became apparent I didn't have any say in the matter. I couldn't understand what the ladies were saying, much less able to plead with them in a language they could understand. I thought maybe their behavior was normal in Ukrainian culture, and perhaps I'd have to let go of my American notion of personal space. After all, I was new to Ukraine, and I didn't want to offend anyone. Looking back now, I know Ukrainians respect the same idea of personal space Americans do. These ladies were just too drunk to care about social norms. I guess social barriers drop across all cultures once enough alcohol is involved.

Thankfully, and by God's grace, their plans were cut short as three Ukrainian policemen slid the door open, again with the force of a tornado. Their statures were towering and stern. They began shouting commands with the vibrato of a boxing match announcer and the delicacy of a raging bull. I must have looked like a deer in headlights when Roman told me the men were demanding everyone's passports and ordering everyone to stand up. In my fear and confusion, my brain lost its ability to command my body's movements, and I sat paralyzed on the edge of my bunk.

As the policemen, Roman, and the supposed hairdressers stared at me, my crippled posture broke as I extended my quivering hand to surrender my passport to the angry men. As soon as my papers were in the policemen's hands, "stupid American" slipped through their teeth in a thick Russian accent as they shoved my documents back towards me. I was delighted to learn these men knew some English, but my excitement quickly turned back to utter fear when it was apparent the policemen were ordering everyone but me out of the room.

Roman again looked to me and quickly whispered "pray" as he was whisked away with the hairdressers. Just like that, I found myself all alone in a foreign country with my interpreter and guide having just been kidnapped by the police. There was again no indication of what I should pray for other than Roman's safe return.

For the next thirty minutes, I sat alone in the matchbox room, wondering what was going on. I continued to pray, but all I could mumble was, "Please God, please God, please God." My mind raced between the possibility of never seeing Roman again and having to figure out my own way to safety in Lugansk. I felt completely helpless as I searched for reasons why my adventure was already off to such a rocky start.

After what felt like an eternity, Roman finally returned. He slowly slid open the door to our room and silently laid down across from me, still wiping away sweat from his forehead and a tear from his eye. I blankly stared in his direction, looking for some sense of hope and relief. His eyes didn't meet mine, and his skin was pale.

Roman collected himself as he sat up and explained someone had reported the hairdressers were drinking in the room. The hairdressers' behavior was illegal and a quick way to get arrested, thrown off the train, or both. The policemen accused everyone in the room of drinking, and Roman begged them to believe him that only the hairdressers were drinking. Thankfully, the hairdressers finally confessed they were the only guilty ones, and the police let Roman go.

As we arrived at the train station in Lugansk, things around us seemed to have calmed a bit. Roman and I had managed to sleep for part of the train ride, and we'd found a meal to eat. When we stepped off the train, Adam was standing there as I remembered him from our dinner together in America. He was smiling cheek to cheek and ready to drive us back to our village, named Novopavlivka, which would become my home for the next nine months. He greeted Roman and me as if we were his own kids and then loaded us up in his old Soviet car. In an instant, everything around me became unfamiliar and exciting, and I knew Adam was there to help me figure things out.

The car bumped and jolted down worn out Ukrainian roads, just like my thoughts and emotions had bounced around my head a few hours before. The old Soviet-era car Adam drove made a grinding sound when he changed gears in the manual transmission, and the windows rolled down with a crank instead of a button. I couldn't help but smile as we passed the unknowns of my new world. The smells and textures of my new home flooded my emotions and senses. During my first car ride in Ukraine, I knew there was much to let go of and much to learn.

Luckily, Roman and I didn't get arrested that day, and we

didn't get new hairstyles, but I did learn a lesson on the train. God used a frightening but also funny journey to teach me that even if I didn't exactly know what to pray for, I could trust Him and His plan. Life is full of times when we don't know what's going on around us or what will come from our situation, but God promises us He won't abandon us. If you're like me, you often forget this truth when it seems we have more questions than answers. There are likely situations in your life, just as in mine, when you feel God is distant and you're left babbling like a child repeating, "Please God, please God, please God." I've learned it's alright to feel helpless sometimes because God's promises never fade, no matter what our circumstances are.

It's incredible to me how many times I can forget God's faithfulness. I sometimes find myself feeling lost and forgotten only to have a friend, or my wife, swoop in with an encouraging word. I know this isn't always true for everyone, so I write these words carefully. The Lord has blessed me with a network of people who genuinely care about me and want the best for me. However, I know the Lord has also positioned people without a safety net. When I reflect on that group of people, I am reminded God alone is sufficient for each of our lives. He doesn't *have* to use those around us, but He sometimes *chooses* to. If I have one word of encouragement in this area, it's this: God is good, and He is loyal. I don't pretend to understand how the Lord uses those around us or how He uses us for others, but I do know one thing. God is faithful, and He won't let go of His people.

No matter your situation, remember this. God will not put you in unbearable situations or ones exceeding your limits. It may be that your darkest hour or most trying time is showing you Jesus is enough. Don't let go and always be alright with praying, "Please God, please God, please God." The Lord knows your heart, and He knows your needs and desires. Trust

Him to sustain you and always look to Him for your next move. Similar to the chaos of my move across the pond, you may feel lost, but remember, God stands firmly on the other side of your journey, holding a sign with your name on it. He'll be smiling the whole time as He eagerly awaits your arrival.

Black Hills

I used to think I had to have a detailed plan of action. Now I know it's sometimes better to simply go.

During my adventure in Ukraine, I lived in a small village on the outskirts of Lugansk called Novopavlivka. I know, it's a mouthful. The village exists in a lonely part of the country, and it's not the kind of place people move to. More often than not, locals search for more suitable places to live instead of inviting outsiders in.

A single paved road connects surrounding communities, but the village roads are unpaved and filled with ruts. Farmland borders the dirt path, and there's a small pond where locals fish for leisure. Apart from a few cows grazing in the middle of the road and the occasional local bus, there's not much traffic on the main village road.

The village itself is in the valley of tall hills, which are polluted with the remnants of old coal mine shafts from decades of illegal mining. I'm sure these coal mines were essential to the nation's efforts in the Soviet days, but they are simply a base level job to locals today. Many of the working-age men who live in the village still work in the illegal coal mines. It's common for the miners to develop what the locals call "black lung" and die at a relatively early age. No organizations or laws protect the working environments for these men, so they are forced to provide for their families at the expense of their shortened lifespans. Periodically, the local police come by and apply fines to these men for working in the mines, but it's all a game. Both the police and the locals know the coal mines will continue to operate, and the police will continue to collect personal donations backed by the power of their badges.

Many of the miners arrive at a bus stop filled with cigarette butts scattered among broken bottles of beer and vodka. It's an unfortunate reminder of the status quo lifestyle in this area of Ukraine. Across the street from the bus stop sits the village's club. I never figured out the purpose of the club as it was most often empty, but it, in fact, has the word "club" written in Russian above the main door. I think "gossip hall" is a more fitting name due to the elderly village ladies who periodically gather there.

Further down the dusty street is a store where locals buy small items like bread, a Coke, and even a full unscaled dried fish. If you put five people in the store, the place would be packed and would have driven an American fire marshal mad. Right outside the store sits an old bench where men and women sit and drink all day long, every day. The store is the village's main attraction, and many locals use it to distract themselves from reality.

Every home is painted with various muted shades of light blue and golden yellow. The Ukrainian flag is blue on top and horizontally split with yellow on the bottom, and it seems a lot of national pride went into the color scheme of the village. A trench divides two rows of houses, and several homemade dinky bridges provide a path to neighboring homes. Everything in the village seems makeshift, and nothing is of modern taste.

The houses in the village are old and broken down. There's a gate and bench in front of each home, and most have a garden suitable for a small family. Many homes have cracks running down the front, and most roofs are missing shingles. Each house has a well as a water source, and almost nobody has an indoor toilet.

As you progress through the village, the condition of homes and the worn-out road further deteriorate. The road's grooves get deeper, and the houses seem to sink a bit further into the earth. I don't think the gradual decline in conditions was by design; the village simply appears to have weathered at different rates. After all, not many people come through the village who anyone feels the need to impress.

Fortunately, I lived towards the beginning of the village, the nicer part. I knew a man named Jing who lived deeper into the village, so I ventured back that way often. Jing was a Chinese man who immigrated to Ukraine, searching for a better life for him and his family over a decade before I met him. Based on his humble house and lack of resources, it's hard to imagine a village in Ukraine being an improvement for him, but he assured me it was. Jing was always smiling and reminded me my temporary venture outside of my comfort zone was an improvement in conditions for others. He seemed content and happy with his life, and his outlook inspired me to be more grateful.

In the summertime, chickens, dogs, cats, and cows congregate in the middle of the village's main road. Shepherds stroll with their livestock and mostly keep to themselves. The entire village feels dingy yet peaceful. There is a particular smell to the village, which is a combination of burning coal and farm animals. It's one of those smells which forever and inextricably ties your mind to an exact location and time, but you can never seem to duplicate it.

The villagers' body language let foreigners know there isn't much movement in or out of the community. It's easy to feel like an outsider. I'm not sure when someone last wandered these village streets without everyone around knowing their name and family history. The people look mostly tired and aggravated. Some greet me, but others frown and act like they have no idea who I am despite how many times we cross paths.

The majority of villagers are elderly and lived most of their lives in Soviet times. In fact, in the many conversations I had with them about their cultural and societal preferences, most seemed to prefer the old days. They told me back then, they didn't have to worry about where their food was coming from or if they would be warm in winter, but I always wondered at what cost these things were assured. The villagers now mostly provide for themselves with their backyard gardens. They grow their crops and save whatever they can for the winter in their underground cellars. Locals keep a log of items bartered and help provide for one another.

I've often considered the origins of the stern face many Ukrainians wear. Maybe it's from a difficult political past, financial hardship, or the long, brutal winters which take their toll over time. I don't know the answer, but I found many Ukrainians have the facade of a stony heart with Jell-O underneath if you are ever allowed to break through the barrier. Their stubbornness and social retreat seem to be a defense mechanism, but I don't suppose that's all too different than Americans can act at times. Every human wants to be loved and heard, and I figured the Ukrainian people were no different. In some ways, their thick walls drove me to a determination to win them over.

When my introverted tendencies needed an escape from life in the village, I would climb the rolling hills and high vantage points which lined the perimeter of the village. If you walked to the tops of the hills surrounding Novopavlivka, you could see the vast countryside for miles. Farmers tending to their work in modest fields scattered your view from above the village. Desolate and distant roads could be traced back to a city named Lotogina, the nearest small town that offered a few more groceries and goods.

The scenery was vague enough to allow my mind to recreate my desired surroundings. Some days I was in Italy, sometimes France or Ireland, but mostly in Alabama overlooking an unassuming landscape. The hilltop became my favorite place in the village to go and be alone, and I went there often to recharge. When I was on top of the hills, I could allow myself to forget about the radically different life awaiting me back in the village. Being on top of the hills cleared my head. I couldn't hear anyone speak in a foreign language, and my mind wasn't filtering every word through its developing translation machine.

The air was different atop the hills, and I could watch the breeze systematically wonder across the tall wheat fields. As I quietly observed the world around me, I was reminded the same sun rises and sets in Ukraine as it did in Alabama. There was something comforting knowing my friends and family thousands of miles away saw the same sun and moon I did. People in surrounding villages still woke up to work their fields just as my dad awoke to work his job back home. There was a certain amount of solace as I remembered the same desires and objectives drove people in Ukraine just as they did in Alabama.

As I learned soon after moving to the village, farmers in the area burn their fields near the end of summer each year. I imagine this is a routine occurrence for the natives of Novopavlivka and farmers alike, but to say I awoke in a panicked frenzy as thick black smoke filled my village would be the understatement of the century. Luckily for my pride, I wasn't the only one panicked. It quickly became apparent something had gone wrong this year, and the fire was quickly spreading much further than the farmers' fields. I'm certainly not an expert in agriculture or farming, but I assume there are certain measures farmers take to prevent fast-sweeping fires. Even in my limited knowledge, it quickly became apparent our village was in trouble. If farmers had taken any steps to avoid a massive and sweeping fire, they had all failed.

If you've ever seen a long fuse being lit leading to a firework, you know the ember travels fast. This scenario was similar, only the fuse was rolling wheat fields, and the fireworks were people's homes. All at once, the entire village realized this fact, and we all were like deer staring into headlights. Finally, our paralyzed shock broke, and all of the villagers sprang into action knocking back the incoming flames with homemade brooms and buckets of water.

I was still relatively new to Ukraine at this point and didn't know much Russian. During the commotion, I didn't know if the locals were speaking their native language or if they had all burst into speaking in tongues. After all of our brooms were burnt and the buckets of water spilled and splashed about, we determined our efforts would be futile and called the firetruck for help. To be honest, I don't believe anybody in the village had any real confidence in the incoming help. At best, the firetruck was conservatively an hour away from us if they didn't stop to have a cigarette and beer first, but it was our only hope.

I don't believe there wasn't an emergency line to call for help. I think it was more of a call to a buddy who happened to have a homemade firetruck. For the sake of understanding this story, I want you to forget any notion you have of a firetruck. It's all wrong. If you've ever seen a volunteer fire department, you should know those guys look like action heroes compared to what we had available. The so-called "firetruck" was a glorified flatbed truck with an actual bathtub strapped to its back. A Dukes of Hazard style red emergency light, which worked after giving it a good thump, graced the vehicle's hood.

After what felt like an eternity, the firetruck finally came bumping and bouncing into sight, and I instantly understood we were in for trouble. The late summer sun evaporated any drop of water, which splashed like small tidal waves over the sides of the bathtub and onto the dusty roadway. The dehydrated clay absorbed water at a quicker rate than a frat house makes beer disappear on a Friday night. I stared at the lazily approaching truck with a blank face and the hopeful doubt this might be a joke. It was almost as if the villagers were saying, "The dumb American is in the village. Let's have a laugh." I was wrong.

As the firetruck stopped just inside the village, the raging fire reminded me this was, in fact, not a joke. By this point, the fire had overtaken two homes and was racing towards the old military base we used as a Christian camp. The blaze didn't seem to overly concern the "firefighters" who arrived in the "firetruck" based on the way they sullied around. I was quickly losing faith in their abilities anyway, so it didn't matter much to me how they acted. Our camp was filled to the brim with Ukraine's youth, and don't forget; the entire camp was a lie! We realized it would be up to us to form a plan of action as the firemen looked to us in a rather bored fashion. It was almost as if the firemen said, "I mean, we brought *some* water to you. What else do you want?" After all, the firemen had shown up, which must have been their only goal, it seemed.

Several of the villagers gathered around to draw up a plan, similar to how you do as a kid designing a trick play for back yard football. We realized we had a large water tank at the camp, which we used to supply the camp dorms and food hall with water. The water tank used a pump to draw water from a nearby well and seemed like a viable water supply option. We thought it would be a decent plan, or more accurately, the only plan to refill the firetruck's bathtub and drive through the village as we hung off the sides, splashing buckets of water towards the fire.

The plan was crude, and nobody knew if it would work, but we were excited to have some chance of escaping death, so we all jumped into action. We knew if we were going to face death, we would meet it with a bucket of water in our hands. Locals gave me the task of operating the electric pump that drew water from the well and into the tank when it ran low. The job seemed like an insult to my perceived abilities, but I was the outsider in the village, so I didn't complain.

We must have looked foolish driving through a burning village, throwing water on the raging flames as if we were having a splash fight at the neighborhood pool. The fire mimicked the prank birthday candles, which keep reigniting each time you blow them out. The flames were taunting us each time we threw water at them. It was infuriating and demoralizing. There was never a time when we noticed a momentum shift in our favor, but the wind seemed to blow the fire beyond our village after a while.

Despite losing two homes in the fire, I have to imagine it was God's grace, and maybe even a miracle, that we didn't lose more. Fortunately, the homes claimed by the fire were vacant and likely beyond repair before the fire. Our camp, where we did most of our daily activities, had been up for grabs in the blaze, but the flames spared it. One thing was made clear, however. I'm not all that good at firefighting, but as it turned out, neither were the firefighters who showed up.

We didn't have a plan for when a fire of this magnitude would break out, and we didn't have the answers in the chaos. Much like my move to Ukraine, our decisions were off the cuff during the fire, and we had no expertise or experience to rely on. All we had was God's faithfulness and each other. I often view my time in Ukraine in the same way, working each day with a general plan at best, but in most cases, working each day with the assurance God wouldn't forsake me.

When I think back to the little firetruck that showed up with no water, I see a picture of a group of firefighters who arrived woefully unprepared. They didn't seem to have a plan, and they didn't even seem interested in the task at hand. To them, the fire was just another problem in their lives. They had no personal connection or investment in solving the issue. To the people who lived in the village, this was their home and their people. The villagers viewed the fire as a threat to safety but also a threat to their livelihoods. The neat part is, God provided an army of people who worked together, encouraged one another, and ultimately others before themselves because the locals were invested in each other's lives. Sometimes opportunities to help and to love are spur of the moment deals. We don't always have the luxury of getting everything in order. It was true for the villagers during the blaze, and it demonstrated the level of support and care they had for one another.

After we extinguished the fires and the firetruck returned to wherever it came from, I sat and observed the villagers. Each of them went door to door, checking on their neighbors, friends, and loved ones. They wanted to make sure they were alright and everyone's needs were met. The closeness of the locals was evident. It made me consider my own circle, not only back in America, but also my growing relationships in Ukraine. Despite their desperation and lack of resources, the villagers looked to those around them first before concerning themselves with their own needs.

Weeks after the fire, I found myself back on top of the hills, looking out across the vast countryside surrounding my village. It was quite a different scenery this time as all of the hills were pitch black and still smoldering. I couldn't help but question if there were any more homes lost across the region or if the farmer who accidentally caused the blaze was alright. As I sat wondering questions I'll likely never have an answer to, I was reminded of God's faithfulness.

As a decade has gone by since I lived in Ukraine, I sometimes look back and question how in the world I was ever naive enough to simply pick up and move across the world without a plan. I've realized God doesn't always require us to have all our plans and resources in order. Sometimes He just says, "Go." In fact, I think God sometimes shakes up our plans intentionally to demonstrate His power over our lives and circumstances. I've found life is richer when I live on the edge of my seat, looking for ways to just go, to be present, and to be willing.

Life has a way of slowly making us feel as if our current situations shackle us. As we grow older, our families grow, more dotted lines have our signature on them, and we tend to feel settled. I'm guilty of this too. But, my hope is we're able to take periodic snapshots of our lives and ask ourselves if we are living up to our God-given potential. We all have something unique to offer this world. Sometimes it just takes the willingness to be uncomfortable and moveable and to just go.

Boxed Milk
God is with us, even when we are buying milk.

Not long after moving to Ukraine, I made friends with an American guy named Steven. He told me he worked for the United States Peace Corp when I asked him why he was in Ukraine, but I never quite understood what he did for them. We met at camp in the village I lived in because he volunteered there in his free time by helping lead worship. My initial draw to Steven was the fact he could speak English, and he had a guitar. He frequently strummed Billy Joel's *New York State of Mind* on his guitar as he sang along, and he had a good voice. At this point in my life, I was obsessed with playing guitar, mostly to the despise of those around me. I was content with knowing only three songs on the guitar, but those around me seemed to wish I knew none.

Steven was an interesting guy. He was filled with stories and experiences that proved he had carved his own path in life. Travel consumed a large part of his life, but he called upstate New York his home. Steven spent a considerable amount of time in a Latin American country before coming to Ukraine, but the reason for him being there is still unclear to me. It was there he learned fluent Spanish, similar to how you or I would learn a new card game. It wasn't long after meeting Steven when I realized he spoke English, Russian, Spanish, and was learning Ukrainian.

He seemed like the kind of guy who quickly picked up things but didn't realize his brain worked differently than those around him. He once told me a Harvard professor allowed him to join his class unofficially when he was living in America. Steven didn't seem to care much about prestigious degrees or titles. He simply desired to learn and felt Harvard was the best place for him to do so. I've always had suspicions of Steven being linked to some secretive agency of the American government. I guess I'll find out after this book is released if I blew his cover.

One day, Steven invited me to stay with him for a weekend in his apartment. He lived within Lugansk's city limits, which was about an hour bus ride from where I lived in the village. Lugansk is mostly an industrial city, one which isn't overly concerned with fancy fixtures or modern trappings. The city itself is relatively monotone and simple. There are long streets lined with small markets and restaurants, but it's nothing like Kiev, Ukraine's more European capital. Instead of glass-front high rises in modern cities, you're more likely to find yourself walking by smokestacks and factories in Lugansk.

Buses clank and bump by filled full of people from all walks of life. It's not uncommon to board a bus and have to stand due to lack of room. Even if there's a seat on the bus, there will almost certainly be an armpit in your face from someone standing and holding onto the overhead rails. People on the street don't wave or smile at strangers, something I learned the hard way. I was instructed by more seasoned people to always carry my bag in a way which allowed me to see it. Otherwise, it's an easy target for thieves. All in all, Lugansk is a tough city. It's obvious to even a casual observer that the city is filled with people who have more creases and lines on their faces than the average person.

When the weekend came for me to stay at Steven's, I was shown which bus went from my village to the city and eagerly hopped on when it came around. After the bumpy Friday-afternoon bus ride, I found myself with some free time in Lugansk since I arrived to the city while Steven was still at work. It certainly wasn't in my best interest to be alone; I virtually had no Russian language skills. I had only been to the city a couple of times, but never by myself. My early arrival was not by mistake, I figured I would use the extra time to explore a bit and have some time to myself. I'm an introvert and being alone recharges me, so I was happy to be solo for a little while.

Once I made it to the city, I was hungry, so I headed off to the supermarket to buy a few items. It never crossed my mind on the way to the store that, at this point, I didn't speak a lick of Russian. I guess my seventeen-year-old brain simply glossed over the fact as I excitedly headed out into the city. I don't know what I was thinking, but then again, it's probably as simple as I wasn't.

After walking for what must have been miles, I began looking for the best store to shop at. As I wandered around, my criteria for selecting a store required an alluring sign, bright lights, and automatic glass sliding doors. As I would find out later, only one store in Lugansk fit my demands, but I found it eventually. I'm sure everything in the store was three times the price as other local shops, but after a few weeks in the village, a little touch of modernity and familiarity was something I badly needed at the time.

As I entered the store, I immediately recognized I had made a monumental mistake. I couldn't understand anyone around me and all of the squiggly lines on signs looked as if someone tripped as they were writing them. "No problem," I thought as I tried to comfort myself, "I'll just pick up the items on my list which look similar to what I'm used to in America." If I had been honest with myself, I would have admitted what I really wanted was a translator, but I was too headstrong for that.

The first item on my grocery list was milk. Intuitively, I found my way to the aisle lined with refrigerated items behind clear swinging doors, just as I was accustomed to in America. I must have made forty or more passes up and down the aisle looking for anything resembling a gallon of milk. To my disappointment, I never found it. I thought for sure I had missed it, but I decided to look for a few more items on my list before returning to look once more, still with an empty cart, for the milk.

Many minutes later, and with no groceries in my cart, I stumbled down an aisle, and something strange caught my attention. In the middle of the canned goods aisle, I saw a white cardboard box, again with some unintelligible squiggly lines. I wouldn't have thought much of it, but I noticed the box had a cartoon illustration of a cow. I must have looked like a fool to anyone watching as I held the box to my ear as I gently shook it.

There was definitely liquid inside, but I couldn't see what was in the box. I ran my finger down the back label of the box, similar to the way you slide your finger down a multiple-choice test after you didn't even attempt to study for the exam. Doing this made me feel a little less like a complete dummy and hopefully tricked other shoppers into believing I could read. After doing this routine a few more times, I gave the slight approving nod any guy does when he has no idea what's going on and decided to put the box in my cart.

I hadn't found a jug of milk, but I did check the refrigerated aisle another five times, you know, just to be sure it wasn't there. After realizing it had taken me over an hour to find what *might* be milk, I decided to count my losses and not even attempt to find the chicken I had on my grocery list. After all, who knows how that would be packaged? Plus, I had to figure out how to pay for my cardboard box with liquid inside, so I headed off to the registers.

As I made my way to the registers, I realized I had to figure out a strategy to preserve some dignity once I was face to face with the cashier. I thought if I acted like I was trying to dig in my pockets to find my money and slowly lay one bill in the cashier's hand at a time, waiting for them to pull away, maybe I could play it off like I knew what I was doing. My thinking was I'd rather be the guy who takes too long rather than the dumb one. One thing I didn't know at the time was every time you go to the grocery store in Ukraine, the cashier asks if you want a bag before they start ringing up your items. I also didn't know the bag costs extra. Of course, this was my first time at the grocery store in Ukraine, and I couldn't have anticipated the question ahead of time.

As I approached the cashier and placed my cardboard box filled with liquid on the counter, the cashier looked at me and plainly asked in Russian, "Do you want a bag?" It was a simple question. I wish I could have seen my face because my plan was already off the rails, and I could tell by the cashier's body language we weren't going to go any further in our interaction until I answered the question. Wide-eyed, I quickly considered all the typical questions like "Did you find everything you need," or "How are you," and even "Do you want to donate money to some cause?"

I figured the most universal answer I could give to her question was, "Okay." So, I nodded my head, smiled, and simply said, "Okay." She was on to me. I could tell by her slight pause and glare at me she must have been thinking I was missing a few screws in my head. Regardless, she charged me for the plastic bag and quickly blurted out what I assumed was the total I owed. Sticking with my original plan, I slowly placed one bill at a time, of the lowest denomination, in her hand until she pulled her hand away. Little did she know, she could have charged me a hundred bucks for that liquid-filled cardboard box.

As soon as she turned to the cash register with my money in hand, I picked up my cardboard box filled with liquid and sprinted for the door. As I ran, I faintly uttered the only two phrases I knew in Russian at the time, "Thank you," and more importantly, "I'm sorry." I must have looked like I had just robbed the place with how fast I was moving while glancing over my shoulder at the cashier. Once I was outside the store, I figured I'd enjoy some sort of relief, but people around me quickly reminded me I didn't yet speak Russian, and that would be a problem exiting the grocery store couldn't fix. All I wanted to do as I exited the store was get back to Steven's apartment and hide. I didn't have enough courage left to figure out the bus system, so I decided I would just walk.

I'm sure a bus ride back to Steven's apartment would have been only a few dollars and likely a heck of a lot faster. In my humiliated state, I figured I would walk the mile or so back to the apartment, praying the entire way someone on the street wouldn't stop me to ask a question. After all, the chances of "thank you" or "I'm sorry" actually making sense to a stranger's question were slim to none, and my pride could take only a couple more beatings until it was completely shattered. The Lord certainly cut me some slack because I found out soon after my trip to the grocery store that Steven's apartment was budget-friendly, to put it nicely, and located on the same partially paved street as a drug rehab facility. This one street was well known for its shady characters and uncapped needles littered about, so my adventure certainly could have been worse.

Steven's apartment was a remnant of the Soviet era. The building itself stood tall with almost no charm. In fact, when I think of Steven's apartment, I'm reminded of the face of a Soviet soldier. They both look bleak and stern, almost uninteresting in their simplicity.

Getting into Steven's apartment wasn't easy. Steven was still at work, but he left me a set of keys. There was a large and heavy metal door that secured the building from the outside world. After climbing many flights of stairs that smelled like urine and vomit, I found myself standing in front of a door with multiple locks. I guess it was nice having several backup locks considering Steven lived directly across the street from the rehab clinic, but actually getting inside his place felt like a magic trick.

The inside of the place wasn't much better than the exterior. Only three tiny and bare rooms made up the entire apartment. There was a bathroom with no hot water, a bedroom, and a kitchen so small that I could touch opposing walls at once with ease.

Once in Steven's kitchen, I placed my cardboard box full of liquid on the table and pulled up a chair to examine it. I'm not sure what I thought would change from my in-store study of the box to now, but I decided to examine it again. I considered the possibility what I had purchased was not actually milk, but returning it was out of the question. For all I knew, I could have just picked up baby formula or coffee creamer. There was only one way to find out, so I opened the box, cautiously sniffed, and took a sip as my lips quivered in anticipation. Good news, it was milk, I think. I'm sure a milk dinner didn't make for a healthy meal, but fear and discomfort dulled any hunger pains I had that evening.

As I sat and drank what I think was milk out of a cardboard box, I started to laugh a little. Looking back at my first grocery store trip, I fell somewhere in the middle of a failure and the mom who cuts coupons to save fifty Dollars at the checkout line.

Sure, I had only milk for dinner that night, but it could have been worse; I could have had coffee creamer. It was little moments like this in Ukraine when I felt most alone and most vulnerable.

I didn't know more than a couple of Russian words initially, and times like this served as stark reminders that I was far outside of my comfort zone. In fact, I was about 5500 miles away from anything resembling familiarity or comfort. All I had was God's promises to lean on. The only thing required of me was to learn, and relearn, His promises were enough.

I now know the word for "milk" in Russian. It sounds a lot like the English word. I also know my adventures in Ukraine opened my eyes to look for little moments, like buying milk, to anticipate God teaching me to depend on Him. Little moments like this stacked up to become a great teacher and an even better pride checker. I didn't need a translator in the grocery store as I thought. What I really needed was to trust God.

It was silly times like these when I felt God coming alongside me, grabbing my hand and saying, "Let's do this together." You see, the entire time I was walking up and down the aisles in that grocery store, God was walking beside me, probably laughing, but reminding me everything would be alright. All I needed to learn was to trust Him. I didn't have to be perfect, and sure, some lessons were more challenging to learn than others, but all I had to do was to continue to trust Him, just as I did when I boarded a plane to Ukraine.

God tells us in His Word that He's always with us. I used to think that meant He's with us in the big-ticket items, like life and death, but now I know He's also with us when we're buying milk. He delights in us looking towards Him for guidance and comfort. All we have to do is trust Him.

I've often found myself questioning my next step in life and denying callings and nudges by God. I'm such a stubborn person, and I sometimes believe God is wrong or is skimping on His duties. It's such a humiliating and humbling thing to realize I don't have the answers nor the knowledge to steer my ship alone. At some points along the way, I've tried naming myself Captain, but God faithfully reminds me I have no control without Him as waves crash into my ship.

Since moving back to the States, I've often found myself, with no language barrier excuse, realizing I messed up and need the Lord's guidance in my life. Whether it be letting my wife down, disappointing my friends, or being utterly lost in whether to turn left, right, or continue straight in life, the Lord has faithfully stepped in and guided me towards Him along the way. I often look back to my time in Ukraine as a placeholder in realizing I continually need God's help. In all His wisdom, the Lord made you and I and continues to guide us as we walk through life. My hope is you too will realize the Lord's faithfulness in guiding you through adversity and questions of what to do next. I don't claim every step won't be met with resistance or questions, but I do know trusting in the Lord will provide the reminder, stability, and comfort that God won't let you down.

Friendship Flag
I used to think "community" was a church buzz-word. I now know the people around me matter.

I turned eighteen not long after moving to Ukraine. By my birthday, I had been living in Ukraine for a couple of months, just long enough to start feeling pretty homesick. I didn't know much Russian, and my relationships with those around me were still in their infancy stage. I was in a strange country far away from the comforts of my own home, friends, and family. To state it mildly, I was feeling pretty depressed as I officially crossed into adulthood.

Instead of being at a summer camp 5500 miles from home, I wanted so badly to spend time with the friends I had been lucky to have since early middle school. Dinner at one of my favorite restaurants would have been welcomed too. I tried my best not to reveal my emotions to those around me in Ukraine. It felt necessary to prove to them, and myself, that I was excited to be in Ukraine, no matter what the circumstances were. Despite my efforts to change the way I felt that day, I walked around feeling pretty down.

I went through most of the day just as I did any other. Apart from the occasional "happy birthday" blurted out in English through a thick Ukrainian accent, there wasn't a noticeable difference in my day. Those around me seemed desperate to keep me busy throughout the day. My friends provided sufficient, yet quiet and unassuming reasons to avoid the room I stayed in during summer camps in the village. I was asked to do odd jobs around camp instead of returning to my room to change clothes or get a snack. It was a bit strange given it was my birthday, but I wasn't going to complain. I was still new.

During camp, all two hundred something kids and staff ate together in a large room. There were community sinks outside of the dining hall style building we shared meals in, and at least a few of us utilized the soap and water before entering to eat. Almost all of our meals consisted of bread, cheese, a whole grain, and some sort of home-brewed fruit juice. Our meals were basic, but I developed an appreciation for our predictably simple entrees. Our meal times at camp became more focused on fellowship and rest instead of Instagram worthy food shots. Meals were simple, and I often shared them with a small group of people who became my friends.

On the day of my birthday, none of my friends said a word about my launch into adulthood. Granted, we were all busy being in the middle of a summer camp, which hosted a couple hundred Ukrainian orphans, but I wished they could spare a measly thirty seconds to sing "Happy Birthday" to me. Regardless of my feelings, the entire day went by with no recognition of another orbit around the sun. I began to feel depressed and even forgotten about as the sun started to set. My hope wasn't to be the center of attention, but everyone wants to feel remembered and thought of from time to time. I didn't care for a huge celebration, party streamers, or even a birthday cake, but I wanted to feel close to those around me for my eighteenth birthday.

As the day came to a close, I, along with most everyone else, was tired from a sun-up to sun-down day at camp. My birthday hadn't offered a break in the rambunctious nature of camp;

instead, everyone carried on as usual throughout the day. I could look at the faces of those around me and tell there wasn't much more they could give. We ran camp at full steam with the understanding that between each two-week camp would be a few days of uninterrupted rest. At the start of each race, we committed our energy to a sprint, not a marathon. With that in mind, we all gave everything we had while camp was in session, and it showed in how we dragged along at the end of each day.

As I left dinner on the night of my birthday, a friend pulled me aside and struck up a conversation that seemed to be headed in a direction I didn't have the energy for. He seemed to be droning on and on about meaningless recaps of various points of our days. Nothing he was saying seemed to have much importance or urgency. It seemed like he just wanted to hear himself speak. At the time, it didn't occur to me he was stalling me, so I gave him the attention and patience I felt I owed him even though I wanted to ask for permission to pick the conversation up in the morning. After a few minutes of innocuous conversation, he abruptly wrapped things up, and we headed our separate ways. As I drifted back towards my room, I considered our conversation's unusual nature but didn't think much of it. I was tired and ready to go to bed.

By the time my friend and I finished our conversation, my other friends had disappeared. I felt a little bummed because I wouldn't get to spend time with them as I had hoped. As I walked towards my room, I imagined what my friends and family were doing back in America and wondered if they had thought of me.

Without any inclination to the fact, the friends I had come to know in my short time in Ukraine were quietly plotting a big eighteenth birthday celebration for me. Like most Ukrainians, once you've broken past their rigid outer shell, the locals around me were incredibly thoughtful and kind and showered me in love and acceptance. I hadn't known my new friends for long, but I trusted they had my interests in mind. They helped me learn to put others before myself and repeatedly demonstrated thinking of me before themselves.

As I entered the small building where my room was located, I didn't suspect anything out of the ordinary. I was still wishful my friends had remembered my birthday, but the building was quiet as usual, and nothing seemed out of place. As I reached into my pocket and retrieved the skeleton key to open my ancient looking door, I was met with a racket and cheer, which shook the walls. The door to my room flung open, and I stood at the threshold in amazement and a bit of shock. My Ukrainian friends, and even a few who were also foreigners, filled my room.

At once, there was a loud celebration and a butchered version of "Happy Birthday" sung mostly in English. Soon after the song came to a train wreck ending, a friend stepped forward and presented a birthday card with a multitude of languages written inside. "Happy birthday" was written in English, Russian, Ukrainian, Arabic, and Chinese, each representing the parts of the world my friends called home. I'm not much of a crier, but the thoughtfulness and kindness of my friends had me close. After I gathered myself a bit, we all sat down around my room and shared a birthday cake and stories of my short time in Ukraine. In that moment, we were family, and we were best friends.

As the evening progressed, one of my friends handed me a small cardboard box that was taped shut. I shook the box and lifted it to my ear to be sure there wasn't a living creature inside. Once I deemed the package safe, I carefully and slowly opened it. Inside was a simple gift. It was a folded Ukrainian flag with signatures and short messages from my friends and even people I didn't know. All of the messages were encouraging and celebratory. Again, the writings were in five languages, which felt like a globe-sized hug.

The message they were sending was clear. Even though we were from various countries, with different languages, cultures, and backgrounds, they were in my corner. It was important to them that I knew they stood with me and celebrated another year in my life and the connection we shared in friendship and salvation. Together, we hung the flag above the pillow on my bed as my friends made sure I knew they loved me.

When my friends left for the night, I slowly closed the door behind them and paused to look at the Ukrainian flag, which now hung above my bed. With all of the signatures, messages, and smiley faces drawn across the flag, I stood back and smiled. I had a sense of pride and gratitude in knowing I was loved and accepted so far away from home. I realized in that moment that I had friends in a foreign country who cared about me and loved me.

It struck me that a group of people went out of their way to plan and execute a moment for me, which demonstrated fore-thought and love in a form fit for eternal memories. The net of love Jesus put in my life was now cast not only in America but also halfway across the world. The friends and family I was accustomed to in Alabama were now wrapped up in the same net with a bunch of foreign strangers turned friends. I could sense God looking at the situation, smirking and quietly reminding me He'd always take care of me.

Even after many years, I still look back to the night of my eighteenth birthday and see God in it. God knows my heart, my struggles, and my desires. He knows yours too. He knew I was in a lonely place that night, and He provided a reminder of not only does He love me, but the people He put around me love me too. I can't help but see God in the faces of each friend who was in my room that night. My friend's faces reflected God's character and thoughtfulness that night. Their smiles, laughter, and joy in seeing me realize they planned my celebration isn't lost on me. I see the Lord's faithfulness and intimate care for me in that moment.

God's Word reminds us not to worry and to rely on Him for all of our needs. I sometimes read those parts of the Bible and selectively choose the things I'm willing to trust God with. My list changes from time to time, but there always seems to be a struggle with letting it *all* go and letting God take my worries and fears from me. It's almost like I have amnesia in the times Jesus reassures me of His promises, and I have to continually learn it all over again. It's a frustrating pattern.

If you're like me, you tend to worry about a variety of things. For some, it's money, a spouse, a job, grades at school, or simply getting through the rest of the day. As I sat in my room staring at the flag my friends had just hung for me, I felt embarrassed and ashamed in my lack of surety that Jesus had my situation in His hands. It's often in times when God goes over the top showing His love when I'm reminded of His promise to keep and care for me. Deep down, I know these things to be true, but doubt is a struggle for many of us, and that's alright. I think God knows this about us and chooses to demonstrate His immense love for us in ways we don't always see coming. I believe He delights in doing this.

Some of you likely have much bigger worries and fears in life than I did in Ukraine on my eighteenth birthday. It may be you don't know how much longer a loved one can hang on in their sickness. Or maybe you struggle with relationships with those closest to you. For others, it's your parents or the cops who give you trouble. If that's you, know God sees those issues too and deeply loves you just as He loves me. I can't tell you how your story works out, but I can say to you however it does, God is in control of it, and He cares immensely about not only the outcome but also how you feel about it. He's on your side, even on the bad days.

I'd be lying if I told you I don't still occasionally struggle with thoughts of loneliness and the sense of being forgotten. I still find myself looking up and wondering if Jesus is taking the day (or the year) off. I get frustrated when I feel God is slacking on His job, but then I remember how vast the divide is between my understanding and His wisdom. Each time I feel distant or forgotten about by God, I eventually hear His footsteps walking towards me. I don't believe He's taking breaks or forgetting about me. Instead, I think Jesus stands peaking around the corner, waiting for me to fully trust Him and run blindly after Him. When I fail to do that, He slips out from cover and runs towards me with His arms stretched out.

We all get busy with life or with school or work. I'm guilty of sometimes getting too wrapped up in the immediate trappings of life that I forget to take time to make those around me feel special in the same way God made me feel special on my eighteenth birthday. In our modern world, our attention is often divided between various things, sometimes all at the same time. We choose to focus on things that don't stand the test of time, even if we convince ourselves they will.

Our time is stretched thin, and we often forgo meaningful interactions with those around us in pursuit of things that really don't matter too much. We choose not to take the time to plan ways to positively impact those around us, just like my friends in Ukraine did. We allow the immediacy of what's buzzing around us to take control of our affections and intentions. I'm certainly guilty of this, and my bet is you are too.

I believe Satan is after our time as much as he is after our souls. His only wish is to devour us any way he can, and sometimes the easiest way to do that is through our attention and time. As our careers or education progress and our problems increase, we tend to focus only on the next task at hand instead of the people and things in our lives that stand the test of time. It's an easy trap and one which is quiet in its approach. If you're not watchful, this angle of attack stands circle around you before you realize, and it's often a fight to get out.

If you're like me, you look back on segments of your life and realize you missed the mark on certain relationships or goals. I wish more than most things I could go back in time and spend more time with certain people who have been a part of my life. For you, it may be a grandparent, childhood friend, or simply the person at your school or office who you no longer have the ability to connect with. The truth is, all of our days are numbered, and our paths sometimes zig-zag in and out of connection with each other. Our lack of intentional pursuit of others leads to regret and "wish I would have" statements.

Choosing to lean into those around us costs us something. It means we have less time for ourselves and less energy to pursue our own desires. Spending time in thought and prayer of how to bring joy to those around us means we are forced to think about ourselves less. When the needs, desires, and affections of those around us get placed above our own, something magical happens. My friends in Ukraine put my name above theirs on my eighteenth birthday and demonstrated a deep love and concern for me, just like Christ does for all of us.

In the grand scheme of my life, the time I was blessed with in spending time among friends in Ukraine was short. I'm fortunate enough to look back now and see many of my friends were much further along in understanding the truths about putting others before themselves. They poured all they had into making me feel loved and appreciated. They were able to look my direction and say, "I want the best for you." I believe God does this too. He looks at you and me and says, "I love you, and I delight in your joy." I hope you and I will continue to learn what it means to invest in those around us and hopefully make them feel loved and appreciated.

As you examine your own life and those who you consider closest to you, I hope you pause and take the time to make them feel special. If you're like me, you sometimes take for granted those who are in your life. It's normally only until they are gone, for one reason or another, when you realize how important and impactful they were in your life. As I progress in life, I hope to continue to learn how to love, invest, and care for those in my life on a deeper, more meaningful level. After all, Jesus made it His mission to love those around Him on a profound level, and if I'm going to follow Him, I could take a few plays from His playbook.

Holy Cow
**I used to be in the business of personal comfort.
I'm now in the unapologetic pursuit of hearts.**

F eeding a lot of people is expensive. Whether you're
feeding a crowd for a birthday celebration or a bunch of
hungry little kids at a summer camp, the expenses
quickly stack up if you're not selective of what you buy. Many
of the kids who went to our summer camps didn't pay anything
to be there. Most of the orphanages the kids came from didn't
have it in their budgets to pay much, so we often excused their
debts. Luckily, we had a network of donors in America to fund
their expenses, so it all worked out in the end.

As we approached the final camp of the year, our food
budget was running low, and we had to figure out how to make
ends meet. Typically, we'd calculate exactly how much food
we'd need for one of our two-week camps, then simply order a
shipment for that exact amount. Our method usually proved to
be cost-effective and reliable, but with a higher than expected
headcount at one of our last camps, we had to get creative.

Most locals in our area relied upon each other to barter for
their food. One family may raise chickens, another a cow, and
some just a few vegetables. As each particular yield was ready
for harvest, villagers would trade and keep a balance for future

harvests. This system was foreign to me as I was accustomed to doing all of my trading at Wal-Mart back in the States.

It was fairly common to notice fewer chickens running around someone's yard, and the cow on the corner which I used to pet abruptly went missing one day. Simply put, villages in Ukraine seemed to be a revolving door for animals, and I tried my best to look the other way when it came time to say goodbye to them. I'm a softy when it comes to animals, and I hated the thought of one of our village animals going "missing."

One day, as I was walking through camp, Adam stopped me and asked if I wanted to tag along for an adventure. The word "adventure" always gets me excited, and I often say "yes" without first asking what I'm being asked to join. For most instances, this is a quality I'm proud of because it means I get to be spontaneous. Other times, it bites me.

I have to believe Adam knew this about me. Given his upbringing in rural Louisiana, he knew exactly what he was asking me to tag along for, and he was delighted. With a grin on his face, he looked at me and said, "Hop in, we're going to go get some food." Without considering what he could have up his sleeve, I jumped in the car, and we headed off to a nearby village.

Adam and his family lived in Ukraine for many years before I even thought about moving there. He was always looking for ways to connect with the locals in our area, and he sometimes got creative in his outreach. In some cases, Adam became a handyman to connect with villagers; other times, he became a taxi driver as an excuse to invest in those around him. Adam's goal was always to share Jesus with the people of Ukraine, and he didn't care much about how he connected with those around him. He simply wanted to spend time with them. I liked Adam for this. He never seemed bothered with how virtuous a task was or wasn't. He just wanted to serve those around him.

Through his networking process, Adam met a man and wife who lived a few villages over from the one we lived in. This particular village wasn't nearly as nice as ours. It didn't have a summer camp in it, nor did it have a little corner store. There wasn't a single home that had running water or any sort of modern conveniences. The people who lived there had it a bit rougher than we did in our village. I think Adam visited this village often by himself in the early days of reaching out to the locals there. It seemed he understood the need to approach them gradually to gain their trust. Although Adam was often loud, he sometimes took a quiet and unassuming approach when he felt it was best.

This particular day at the end of summer was incredibly hot. It was the middle of August, and the sun seemed to be relentlessly beaming down on our shoulders. The air was dry, and so were the dirt roads which led out of our village. As we bumped and bounced down the road in our old Soviet-built car, we had the windows down and the A/C blasting even though it felt like a hairdryer blowing in our faces. The car had a manual transmission, and the clutch had seen better days. Each gear change was met with a jolt and a headrest slapping the back of my neck. The longer we drove, the more dust filled the car became, and the more we coughed. Rolling the windows up would have solved the dust problem but created the looming threat of a heat stroke. Nothing about our car ride in the summer heat was pleasant, but we were on an adventure, and that made me happy.

After turning out of our village, we took unfamiliar roads which twisted and curved towards our destination. The scenery I was accustomed to faded into an unassuming landscape, and none of the roads or landmarks were familiar to me anymore. After what seemed like hours, we finally rolled into the village Adam had been guiding us towards. As we pulled in, I began to wonder where the store or the restaurant was and began to consider the possibility of having misunderstood Adam.

The village streets offered nothing food related. All I could see were the same dilapidated houses and tired faces that my village had. It seemed unexpected visitors like ourselves were cause for a break in the tasks which occupied the villagers' days. I sensed the village was usually quiet, and its residents didn't anticipate many visitors. The people who were outside stopped and turned towards our car. Most locals seemed to recognize Adam and wave to him as our car bumped and clunked down the dusty village street. Others looked more intently towards the passenger seat of the vehicle.

I began to sense Adam had pulled one on me when I noticed him glancing my way more and more often from my peripheral. Adam's plans seemed to be going just the way he intended, and we were nearing the part where my response became the fuel for his laughter. I delayed looking back at him in the hopes of not encouraging his delight in messing with me, but the time came when it was obvious we weren't headed to a restaurant or store.

As we made a left-hand turn into the driveway of a pale blue village home, I finally looked over at Adam with what must have been a look of disgust and horror on my face. He sensed my discomfort and began uncontrollably laughing as he exited the car to greet the man who was walking out from behind the house. As the emerging man wiped blood from his hands with an old towel, Adam extended his hand to greet his friend. It was clear Adam wasn't concerned as he walked into the man's back yard, but I sat still in the car for a few more minutes, trying to figure out what I should do next. I looked over at the driver's seat of the car and realized Adam left the keys in the ignition. I briefly considered stealing the vehicle. That idea was squashed when the thought of spending the rest of my days in a Ukrainian prison flashed across my mind. I figured Ukrainian prisons didn't have restaurants either.

After gathering courage sufficient for battle, I stepped out of the car and crept towards the back of the house where Adam was. I was careful to quietly step as to not give my position away. As I took my post on the back corner of the house, I carefully peeked around towards the two men. As I bladed my body towards the back yard, I searched my brain for any escape option I hadn't yet considered.

What I saw next will be burned into my memory for the rest of my life. A large tree and a doghouse stood next to a vicious-looking dog on a leash anchored to a metal stake in the ground. Thankfully, the dog was too preoccupied to notice me. If you have the picture of the dog from *The Sandlot* in mind, you're on the right track. The back yard itself was dusty and bare, just like the roads Adam and I just traveled, and it was obvious the guard dog was not selective on where it used the restroom.

As the fear of being eaten by this attack dog rushed through my body, I was quickly distracted by my body's involuntary reaction of swatting the flies swarming my face. As my hand made contact with more flies than I could count, I saw the large cow hanging upside down from a tree in the yard. It quickly became apparent the flies landing on me had just feasted on the cow, which was being butchered by the mystery man in the summer sun. I can't be sure, but I believe every single fly in Ukraine was in attendance that day.

My mind began to connect the dots of Adam's previous comment of getting some food with what was now in front of me, and my body began to show me how well my gag reflex worked. As my body convulsed in what must have looked like a mini seizure, Adam and the mystery man were bent over laughing at me. It was clear the mystery man was the village butcher had been working on this cow for several hours by the time Adam and I arrived, and he was getting close to needing our help. He had managed to pre-package some of the beef and placed it conveniently on the ground on top of some old newspaper. However, the real haul was going to take mine and Adam's help as the backyard butcher cut it from the cow.

As Adam and the butcher studied my reaction, their laughter grew to a hysterical level. After what felt like several minutes, their roar trailed off, and the three of us were left staring at each other in silence. I quickly realized my options were running thin, and I'd soon be expected to help finish cleaning the cow.

I'm not a quitter, and more importantly, I had couldn't get back to my village without Adam, so I decided to pitch in. After a few hours of hacking, sawing, and cutting, we had our portion of the cow packaged and ready to put into our car. As we neared the time to load our car, I looked around, thinking we'd use coolers and ice to transport our portion. I was wrong. The butcher made the first move as he opened our trunk and laid out more newspaper. I think he believed newspaper was surgical grade antibacterial packaging the way he relied on it for cleanliness. Not wanting to cause a fuss, I began to hoard meat into the back of the car. After several minutes of stacking meat into our heat locker of a trunk, the butcher slammed the lid closed and patted the car with a sense of accomplishment and approval.

Before leaving, Adam took a few short minutes to chat one on one with the backyard butcher. I remained at to our car to collect myself. As I sat in the passenger seat, I quietly observed Adam and the butcher standing outside. I don't know which words were exchanged between the men, but their body language insinuated a more heartfelt conversation. Adam wasn't a stranger to resting his hands on someone's shoulders to pray with them, and this was a time fit for that. After their brief conversation, Adam slipped the butcher some cash for the meat and shook hands as they parted ways.

With the back of our car now weighed down and sitting much lower than the hood, the ride back was sure to be even more unpleasant than before. I didn't care much about the quality of the ride; my mind was more occupied with forming plausible reasons of why I had decided to become vegan. The now rotting meat in our sweltering trunk screamed Mad Cow Disease and episodic violent illness. I wanted to forget everything I'd just witnessed, but my mind wouldn't release me.

Adam and I didn't talk much on the return trip back to our village. He was thinking of the conversation he'd just had with the village butcher, and I was reflecting on how my life had been good but was soon to be over if I had to eat the meat we'd just picked up. After a while, we pulled back into the summer camp in our village, where a small team of people met us to help transfer the meat from our trunk to the underground cellar located behind the camp's kitchen. I don't remember Adam nor I explaining where we got the meat from, and nobody seemed concerned about it. Given a chance, I would have gladly sounded the alarm to prevent mass casualties, but I was too tired and emotionally spent after our trip, so I decided to be alone for a while.

I don't know if it was God's providence or simply my mind playing tricks on me, but the meat Adam and I bought from the backyard butcher seemed to last for an unreasonably long amount of time. I prayed for the unsuspecting people eating any dish with beef in it, and I became a vegetarian until I was sure the cow we bought was long gone. To my knowledge, nobody who ate the cow became sick, which only points towards accepting the fact the Lord works in mysterious ways.

I learned a valuable lesson that day with Adam and the butcher. Adam didn't want to eat the meat we bought from the village butcher any more than I did, but he was purpose-driven in his decision to buy it. As I recount the interactions between Adam and the butcher, I realize Adam was going after his heart, not the cow he was selling us. I don't know exactly how long Adam had been visiting the butcher's village before buying the cow from him, but I know Adam had been after his trust. Buying the cow was simply another stepping stone in achieving that.

When I think of how Jesus interacted with people while He was on earth, I see a similar pattern in how Adam treated the butcher. Just like Jesus, Adam wasn't too concerned with comfort or common approaches to problem-solving. Adam knew there were other ways to get meat for our village camp, and many of those ways likely made more sense. But, he saw a need deeper in the butcher than food. Over time, Adam understood gradual approaches with the village butcher could amount to something much more significant than feeding our camp. Buying the cow was just another way Adam could be face to face with him in hopes of displaying Jesus.

What I learned during the late summer trip with Adam to buy the backyard butcher's cow was far more edifying than the protein the cow could have provided my body. I was too caught up in the moment then, but I now realize how profoundly Adam impacted my life when he humbled himself before the butcher. Now, I see people as opportunities to serve and love. Not each person I meet will be easy to serve or love, but I now better understand how Jesus loved those around Him.

I often feel the desire to take the easier and more comfortable route when dealing with people. If you're like me, many people in your life are easy to deal with, and you even look forward to spending time with them. You can also probably think of a few who require a little more effort and courage when interacting with them. As I go through life, I see a lot of people

I'd rather not deal with. Sometimes it's not convenient. Other times I'm simply too lazy or too busy to offer a helping hand to those around me. I think we all share certain attributes in this arena, and it often takes a determined effort to fight against those natural tendencies.

Jesus says He loves His children. That means He loves you, your neighbor, your boss, your school principal, the cop who gave you a speeding ticket, and the homeless man you drive by in your car. If you read accounts of Jesus dealing with people on the fringe of society, you'll see He dealt with lepers and criminals, the sick and poor, and also the dirty and destitute. Jesus didn't seem to be too concerned with what was normal or comfortable when dealing with those around Him. He simply knelt down and welcomed them.

As I look back, I now see how Adam was going out of his way to love the locals. We could have bought meat elsewhere, but Adam was building a lasting relationship with the village butcher. Sometimes we have to be uncomfortable to be trusted and accepted, but if it's for Christ, it's worth it. Maybe this translates to how you treat the people around you. After all, Jesus had a way of humbling himself to meet with those around Him, and I think we could all learn a lesson from His example.

Deep Splinter
I used to think others had to see me being obedient to God for it to matter. Now I know it's only Christ who matters.

Learning to serve others is something that has not come easily to me in life. I know it sounds weird to read that. After all, the entire point of my adventure in Ukraine was to serve others, mostly people I didn't personally know. The roots of my natural disposition stem from a mixture of laziness and the tendency to think of myself before thinking of others. It's an awful way to live life, and it's something I continuously have to course-correct as I evaluate my life's trajectory.

I think many people suffer from the same ailments I do in that regard, but I sometimes wonder if we look hard enough for ways to change those tendencies. Lucky for me, I didn't have the choice in Ukraine to stay stuck in my ways because I became a member of Team Hot Water as the resident woodchopper at camp. Knowing my shortcomings, I have to believe God picked this job specifically for me on purpose.

If you are wondering, my job was every bit as unexciting and non-glamorous as it sounds. The old Soviet-era military training grounds we utilized as our Christian camp for kids hadn't been considerably updated since it was built decades before. Being at camp was kind of like having a window back in time. The camp did not have any water heaters, so it was up to Team Hot Water to provide.

Most homes in the village had a well with a hand crank and a bucket to get water, but we were fancy and had a well with a pump at camp. If we wanted hot water, we had to heat it ourselves in large vats which hung above a makeshift wood-burning furnace. Although heating the water was hard work, I was thankful the camp was one of the few places in the village that had hot water at all. There was nothing fancy or modern about our heating system. The only thing we had to do to keep the water hot was keep the stove burning. It sounds simple, but it was hard work.

The boiler room was in the same building as the showers, so the showers got the hottest water of anywhere in the camp. It was a known rule that you should test the water before jumping into the shower unless you wanted third-degree burns. On countless occasions, I quickly swiped my hand at the running water as I got ready to shower only to be hit with scalding water as another log was thrown on the fire before I committed my entire body to the stream. It was a frustrating mistake, but my gratitude for hot water outweighed my red skin.

The shower and boiler room were located at the back of the property. The facility was just in front of the wood-line next to a small river which twisted through camp. Having the boiler room so close to the wood-line was useful for gathering wood to feed the fire, but it was less than desirable for being close enough to other humans to interact with. Being in the boiler room meant I was distanced from all other activities at camp. It could be a lonely place to be, even for an introvert like me.

As you can imagine, heating water for the entire camp with hundreds of kids running around was a daunting task. Team Hot Water would often set up clandestine patrols to check all the sinks and showers to make sure someone didn't leave a faucet running. In our case, a few running faucets made for an uphill battle in our quest to provide water temperatures greater than a Siberian snowmelt. We were a few dollars short of being able to afford the clear earpieces and black suit jackets like the Secret Service wears, but we imagined wearing these things each time we set out on patrol.

Our operation was relatively simple. We didn't have any modern machinery, like a chainsaw, to aid in our efforts. We simply had several worn-out axes, wedges, and sledgehammers to split wood and feed the hungry fire. It seemed we were constantly running out of hot water, but we gave it our all, and sometimes more. Generating hot water for the camp was an invisible job until, of course, there was no hot water. Then we were in the spotlight.

Team Hot Water was comprised of three full-time guys. Mr. Tony, who you will meet in a few chapters, was a brief member of our prestigious outfit, and he was a welcomed fourth hand. As one guy chopped wood, another would gather and stack trees, and the third guy would feed the fire. We were living large when Mr. Tony was with us because he acted as the helper for whichever guy was struggling to keep up.

During my assignment to the prestigious Team Hot Water, I first began to recognize and wrestle with my laziness and selfishness. I realized my job was to stand out of sight of anyone not associated with my task and chop wood all day long. I mean, how boring is that? The thought of being 5500 miles away from home just to chop wood and feed a stove often ran across my mind.

I sometimes questioned if I was being punished for something or if I had totally missed the mark in thinking my time in Ukraine would be exciting and fun. I watched others use the gifts God gave them to lead Bible studies, play music on stage for the entire camp, or rally a soccer team to win the

Novopavlivka Village Title. But, there I was, chopping wood. The whole thing felt demoralizing and laughable.

Each exhausting day ended with dark soot on my face and blisters on my hands. Those markings were the only telling sign that I had participated in any role at camp each day. It was strongly advised by everyone else at camp that Team Hot Water take a few minutes to wash up before joining everyone else at dinner inside. I don't blame them, though. Most days, we'd show up to dinner smelling like a campfire and sweat. On the days when we were too tired to be bothered or just simply forgot, there seemed to be a social divide that kept us at arm's length from anyone not on the team. The job certainly wasn't one which received any amount of glory or praise, but it meant people had hot water for showers and washing their hands. That was it.

One day as I was chopping wood, I decided gloves weren't needed to do the job, and I'd be more comfortable without them. Like with any group of guys doing manual labor, testosterone was in abundance, and so were egos. After all, I had built a few calluses up at this point, and I was a hardened worker. My confidence, I quickly figured out, was a mistake. I was accustomed to painful blows as the ax slid across my palms when I had an occasional bandaged blister, but I wasn't prepared for what was about to happen.

Over time, I found myself more comfortable with my axe aiming skills and opted for power and strength instead of carefulness in landing the axe in the center of a log. One day as I lifted the axe above my head and slammed it down through a piece of wood, I experienced a moment where I knew I was hurt but not yet sure how badly. It was one of those times you feel pain but prolong looking at your injury until you have mentally prepared yourself. My palm was throbbing in pain, and I could feel the warm trickle of blood running down my hand. After I finally got the courage to look down at my hand, my suspicions were correct. I seemed to have implanted a jagged shard of the old wooden axe handle into the palm of my hand. This was a bad situation, and I immediately knew the splinter would be more painful coming out than it had been going in.

Like most people, I had experienced splinters before, but this was more of an impalement than a splinter. I knew splinters have the natural tendency to fan out and swell once they are inside of your hand, and this one indeed followed course. The wood was so deep in my hand that the color and shape of it faded away under my skin. I could see the top, but I knew most of it was below the surface. It was like an iceberg emerging from the ocean. If the Titanic could have fit into the palm of my hand, it would have crashed again on the wood sprouting from my hand.

Luckily, our camp had a nurse. To be honest, I use the term "nurse" lightly. She wore a white lab coat and had a stethoscope hanging from her neck, but I was a "doctor" for three years in a row for Halloween as a kid, and I wore the same thing. I'm not sure she knew any more than I did about medicine. She worked in a white single-wide trailer that had a red cross crudely spray-painted on the side. It was the antithesis of the prestigious Mayo Clinic.

The nurse seemed to be proficient at taking little kids' temperatures, but a little less helpful when hands-on medical treatment was necessary. American donors regularly sent over-the-counter medicine to help with the camps, and our nurse thought Benadryl, or as she pronounced it, "Bean-a-drill" was the cure for everything. In all fairness, she couldn't read what the label said, so I can't fault her for prescribing it to situations that clearly didn't call for a dose of Benadryl. Unluckily, I found the nurse's limitations when I paid her a visit looking for a remedy for the tree branch sprouting from my palm.

As she carefully looked my wound over and made a few painful pokes and prods, she simply shrugged her shoulders and said she didn't know what to do as she passed me the Benadryl. It's precisely what I didn't want to hear. I was in the middle of a foreign country, in a remote village, and there I was with a splinter so deep in my hand that I'm pretty sure it had roots. If I was sure of one thing, it was Benadryl wasn't going to do much for me.

After exiting the trailer, I sat alone outside and contemplated my next move for what seemed like an eternity. I, too, poked and prodded at my palm, but each touch was met with agony and regret. It was clear the tree branch couldn't stay in my hand forever, and I didn't sense any hope of seeing an actual doctor. I decided I'd do the next best thing—self-administered surgery.

With the nurse's permission, I returned to the trailer and rummaged, one-handed, through all the medical supplies she had to offer. She had quite the collection of bandages and ointments, but a few items caught my attention—hand sanitizer, tweezers, and a pair of small scissors. After retrieving these items, I again sat alone for what seemed like another eternity. I quietly made my peace with the world and asked God to remind my family back home that I loved them.

In my mind, I had already determined I would have to cut the wood out of my hand, but I hadn't yet convinced my working hand to do the task. It dawned on me that I had no idea where the scissors or tweezers had been before I found them. It seemed inevitable I would surely die of an infection soon after removing the splinter from my hand. With that in mind, I knew if I was going to die, I didn't want to die with an entire tree in my hand, so I mustered the courage and got to work.

I started slowly pouring hand sanitizer into the wound in the off chance I could avoid infection. My body quickly let me know the hand sanitizer was doing its job as the palm of my hand turned into the center of the sun. I began to contemplate living the rest of my life with only one working hand and convinced myself it wouldn't be that bad. Amputation is painful, I'm sure, but it was a close second in terms of options.

Team Hot Water needed me back in the saddle, so I figured I would have to toughen up and do what had to be done. I imagined my tombstone reading "Man with a Tree in His Hand" and decided that didn't sound too memorable and knew I had to press on. Again, with no success, I poked and prodded the splinter. It was again obvious the scissors and tweezers would have to come into play.

I started small, snipping away parts of the splinter which were above the skin. I again heavily considered not using my injured hand for however long it would have taken the wooden shard to be naturally forced out of my hand, but I decided that was probably not the best course of action. After many long conciliatory breaths, I made the first snip into my palm. My brain received the signal of intense pain and quickly reminded me I was doing this without any sort of localized anesthesia.

As the tears welled in my eyes, I made another snip and another after that. I don't know what hurt more, the small incisions I was making or the hand sanitizer which dripped deeper and deeper into my palm. Nonetheless, I finally had enough of the splinter exposed to pull it free using the tweezers.

If you have ever played the game Operation, you have a general sense of the precision needed for my next step. I'd be lying if I didn't consider going to the local store to join the drinkers out front for a little bit of liquid courage. Sweat poured down my face, and I mentally prepared myself for my next move. My right hand shook, gripping the tweezers as my left hand winced in anticipation of the painful extraction. I imagine

I had the same amount of fear and worry as someone kneeling over a bomb, praying they cut the correct wire.

I finally mustered the courage to pull the remaining wood out of my palm. As blood poured out and the hand sanitizer dripped even further into my palm, I had conflicting emotions of victory and sorrow. It sounds somewhat heroic and masculine to say I cut the splinter out of my hand but make no mistake, my face and hesitation at the time reflected the polar opposite.

Finally, my hand was free of the splinter that had impaled me. I had been able to save my hand from amputation, and it shook in pain and excitement. I was sure the hand was a definite loss just moments ago, but hope was now on the horizon. I looked around, trying to look tough and courageous, but I really just wanted to cry. I was careful not to make eye contact with anyone around me because I was sure they had just seen me in my state of desperation and were watching to see me realize how minor my injury had actually been. I was just glad to have escaped the one-handed life ahead of me; I didn't need any further trauma in my life at this point.

Needless to say, I took a few days off from chopping wood, but I ended up learning something valuable that day. If you're like me, you might think missionaries are out there being the lead pastor of a village church or evangelizing entire cities. In reality, my experience was much different. I have to admit, I had grand visions at times of impacting large groups of people, but I learned it doesn't amount to a failure to play a more humble role. In reality, I was often in positions like being on Team Hot Water, doing modest tasks with nobody watching.

I learned it's alright to be the guy who doesn't get the attention or the accolades for the things he does. In fact, I like to think of my role in life, and during my adventure in Ukraine, as a supporting actor in a major film. Jesus is the star; I've just been cast to help provide some context for His glory. The best part is,

Jesus doesn't need my help to accomplish His mission, but He includes me. He includes me so I can watch Him change hearts and lives, comfort the hurting, heal the sick, and love His children. All I have to do is follow Him. Sometimes that means following Him to Ukraine, but most times, that means following Him in my office and home.

I'm sure if Jesus kept a report card, I'd have less than satisfactory marks a lot of the time. Thankfully, His grace is better than my effort, and His love is greater than my ability. Jesus knows our hearts and sometimes designs opportunities for us to grow given our current disposition. Looking back, I understand the Lord knew I had a lot of growing to do in the humility department. I don't think it's by mistake that He placed me in a role to quietly serve others.

I didn't know it at the time, but all the wood chopping I did in Ukraine pointed my life towards Christ in a way being in the spotlight could not have. I sometimes wonder what would have happened if I had the prime-time spotlight of ministry in Ukraine. Unfortunately, I think it would have gone to my head, and I would have excused Jesus from the room. Along the way, Jesus has taught me to be humble and to eagerly await the chance to quietly serve someone around me.

I'm thankful for that lesson. I believe it's made me better and I think a similar lesson could make you better too. If you ask me today to participate in the smallest task, I'd like to think I'd jump out of my seat to help. It's not about us; it's about Jesus. Sometimes an axe and a humbling pile of wood can bring more glory to God than a microphone in the spotlight. Just follow Him.

House Key

Look for the small things that can change someone's life.

During the middle of my adventure in Ukraine, an American family proposed I tag along for their adoption of five kids. The idea was I would follow them around and document their journey via video and photos. I had an interest in this sort of creative outlet, but to assume I could transform their journey into meaningful footage was hopeful at best and a disaster-in-the-making at worst. The job seemed so invasive and personal, and I certainly didn't have a resume reflecting any skills for documentary work. Plus, this family asked me to live full-time with them during their adoption journey, which meant I'd see the good, bad, and the ugly. The thrill of witnessing five kids getting adopted was too good for me to pass up, so I tossed aside my fear of screwing the whole thing up and accepted the job.

This family had the opportunity to meet the kids they were pursuing in adoption two years before their trip to Ukraine. In fact, they somehow worked out a deal to have the five kids to their home in America for an entire summer just a year before. That summer proved to be a time where close bonds were created, and the complex emotional roots of these children finding a family began to form. Thankfully, the kids' prior interactions with their soon-to-be parents lessened the growing pains of becoming a family, but that didn't mean the transition was entirely accepted or final.

Fortunately, I had been able to interact with the group of Ukrainian orphans when they spent a summer in America. It wasn't apparent these kids weren't the biological extension of these soon-to-be American parents to the casual observer. Well, except for the whole language gap thing, but we'll gloss over the never-ending game of Charades, which kept everyone entertained and guessing. By the end of the summer, it became evident a connection had formed between the kids and the adults. Christ's love demonstrated it has no language or cultural barriers. It simply finds us where we're at and clings to us.

Despite allowing several of their kids to visit America the summer before, Ukraine had some rather strict rules regarding our visits to these kids in the orphanage. I never could quite reconcile the reasoning for such vastly different interactions, but I think it has something to do with us knocking on *their* doors and asking to come in. Our visits with the kids felt like the orphanage officials were forcing us to dip our toes in the water initially, but we just wanted to dive in and forget about the goggles and snorkels. We were bound to get some water up our nose and be caught leaning over the side of the pool, coughing and gasping for air, but we just wanted to be all in with the kids.

In the beginning, we could only come by the orphanage for a short amount of time, and stern faces in the shadows closely watched our interactions. Each hug felt like it required a quiet permission-granting nod from a shadowed figure standing in the corner. Like anywhere in the world, some love in abundance, and there are others you wonder when and how they lost their affection. This orphanage had both types of people in its leadership, and it was both encouraging and crushing.

There was one caretaker in particular from the orphanage who still brings a smile to my face today. This lady was a bit large in latitude, and she couldn't pass up an opportunity for a hug. Her hair was short and curly, and she always wore a smile. I felt at ease around her. Her personality made me feel good just by sharing the same room with her. She didn't speak a lick of English, but she insisted on being called "Big Mama." I'm not sure she understood what that meant, but she adored being called that, especially by Americans.

Big Mama showed genuine care for the kids in the orphanage. You could tell she wanted the best for them. Still, she also understood the grim reality that many of the kids would be released into society at the age of sixteen without the skills necessary for life on the outside. I think Big Mama knew her time with the kids was short in the grand scheme of their lives, and she seemed to pack as much into each interaction as possible. The kids loved Big Mama, and it was good to have her on our side.

For several weeks, the family I was working for would spend every waking minute juggling the legal side of the adoption as quickly as possible so they could spend the majority of their time loving on their soon-to-be kids. Our days were spent half in stuffy rooms with lawyers and government officials and the other half in the orphanage with a bunch of kids running around and screaming. Each day our relationship with the kids progressed so did our bond of trust with the orphanage staff. Our only goal was to love the kids as genuinely as possible and remind them someone was fighting for them to have a family.

Little Katya and Little Ivan, two of the kids being pursued for adoption, were raised by their biological mother for a short time. One day, their mother took them to a hospital and abandoned them with the lie of, "I'll be right back," only never to return. To make it even worse, it was Little Ivan's birthday the day their mother left them. They were fed false hopes that their mom would come back, even though their mother was suspected of being an alcoholic and homeless with no intention of ever returning. I have to imagine it hurt their mother to leave them, but maybe she felt she had no other choice. No matter the reason, the sad reality was two little children were now in an orphanage with not a lot of hope in their future.

For years, Little Katya was fed lies by people tasked with her wellbeing. She was told the American family wanted to adopt her to induct her into a cult and harvest her organs for some unknown purpose. She was led to believe she'd be betraying her country if she left for an American family. Needless the say, these claims were outrageous and upsetting. They only served as a sad way to instill fear and control over a young orphaned girl.

Little Ivan was a young and energetic boy who loved those around him only the way a child can. He didn't question motives or try to figure out people's angles. He just loved. His love was infectious and brought a lot of joy to the people around him, especially me. Little Ivan and I would sit and chat for hours as we played games. I admit, talking with him was a nice change of pace because he spoke more on the level of my Russian language skills than some of the older kids did. Whenever I visited the orphanage, it was rare to not have Little Ivan by my side.

At the end of the long adoption process, the kids had the opportunity, one by one, to accept or deny the adopting family. The whole thing seemed like something you'd see on Donald Trump's show *The Apprentice*, but the ramifications for these kids' lives were immense. This acceptance process all happened in a courtroom in front of a judge holding a gavel. The air was stuffy, and there seemed always to be a lump in my throat when I stood in this particular courtroom. I didn't bring a suit to

Ukraine, and I didn't want to spend money to buy one, so I stood in the back wearing jeans and a t-shirt. I wasn't trying to be someone I wasn't in this courtroom; I just wanted to see the kids have a brighter future.

All signs pointed towards all five kids agreeing to be adopted, but Little Katya had an abrupt change of heart and was suddenly dead-set on staying in Ukraine. This revelation was heartbreaking and shocking. Options for orphans in Ukrainian society were slim, but she had a way out if she would choose it. Even as a young guy, I could see how Little Katya's decision to stay in Ukraine would be one that had a higher chance of leading her down a dark road. When she refused her adoption, it broke my heart twice because I knew she was also saying "no" for Little Ivan. Ukrainian law said adoption could not separate siblings. Little Ivan was too young to fully understand what was going on, so I decided I'd fight for him.

In our state of shock, the American adopting mother, Victoria, and I hatched a plan to win over Little Katya. We thought if she had something she could keep, something tangible she could hold onto that reminded her of her time with a family in America, maybe she would change her mind. Victoria asked if I had a house key to give to Little Katya. I thought it was a strange request, but I happened to have the key to my parents' house in America in my pocket.

Victoria told me a house key represents a family, security, and love. I had never thought of it, but it's true. I had brought my house key to Ukraine on purpose. There was something comforting to me about having my house key in my pocket. I felt safe knowing I had somewhere to go back to if things went wrong in Ukraine. My house key represented a promised return to my family, familiarity, and love. I hesitated to give it away, but I realized if it meant so much to me, maybe it could mean something to a little girl who didn't have a home or a family. I could only hope and pray my house key would help Little Katya change her mind for her sake and Little Ivan's.

We spent the next day trying to comfort and love Little Katya in a way the people who had been feeding her lies had willfully neglected. I prayed God would speak to Little Katya's heart. Big Mama patiently sat with Little Katya for hours and explained the people trying to adopt her had her best intentions in mind. I don't know all that was said, but I know their conversations ran the gamut of emotions. It was clear Little Katya didn't trust the idea of love or embrace. Why would she? She lived her life as a victim of lies and mistrust, so it was easy to see why she was hesitant to embrace the idea of a family. Regardless, Little Katya so eagerly embraced the affections of Big Mama, and it was clear she wanted love in her life. Even still, Little Katya's heart had become calloused at a young age, and it was going to take patience and work to break through.

Big Mama was trying to convey in words what Victoria and I were trying to convey in action. After hours of pleading with Little Katya, orphanage officials said it was time for us to leave for the day. As the sun went down that evening, it felt symbolic of the fading hope I had in the situation. None of us got much sleep that night. The magnitude of the situation weighed heavily on all of our shoulders, but I can only imagine the confusion and fear Little Katya felt when she laid down in her bed that night. It was unfair for such a young kid to be forced to wrestle with which story was the truth. The cruel reality was Little Katya had to ultimately decide which path was best for her and her little brother. No kid should ever have to do that.

While the sun rose the next morning, we continued to pray. It was difficult not to allow the balloon of hope to swell up inside because I knew a needle-sharp "no" from Little Katya was still possible. As the time came to go back to the orphanage, I don't remember anyone making a lot of noise. The crisp morning air seemed to penetrate deeper into my bones. Our commute was mostly in silence, with the occasional glance towards each other in hopes of relief. Time seemed to move slowly, and thoughts of whether we'd done enough raced through my head.

As we entered the orphanage that morning, I had the same reluctant sense I get when I walk into the dentist's office. I knew what I was about to experience had the strong possibility of being painful, and I wanted to get it over with. As we turned down the long hallway to Big Mama's office, we walked to her closed door. Finally, after a long pause, the door slowly crept open.

Little Katya was sitting inside with Big Mama. As I studied Little Katya's and Big Mama's faces, we shared a collective and tearful smile. After another long pause, Little Katya said "yes" in English. She agreed to the adoption. I think using the language her new parents spoke was her symbolic way of embracing her new life. All I could think was, "Praise God, praise God, praise God" and smile as the orphanage gave Victoria's family permission to take Little Katya and Little Ivan from the orphanage that day.

As I walked out of Big Mama's office, I looked over to thank her. She was sitting with her head in her hands, crying. I could tell the kids meant something to her, and she was glad two more kids now had a family who would love and care for them. Big Mama never stopped pursuing those kids in love and affection. She took the time to bend down and whisper to those kids, telling them someone loves them and wants them. She made sure those little kids knew they were worth being pursued and cherished.

I'm not so sure Big Mama's response was all that different from God's. Just like Big Mama did for Little Katya and Little Ivan, Jesus often sits with us and reminds us we're loved and wanted. If you're like me, it's often our rejection of God that clouds His love for us. We too often choose to listen to lies that confuse and damage our souls rather than trust God's voice in our lives.

By the end of this family's adoption process, I handed the American family hours of video footage and hundreds of photos. I have no idea what came of what I captured on camera, but the truth is, I don't really care. The lasting impact capturing their adoption process had on me was far more valuable than I could have imagined in the beginning. My job was to anticipate moments worth remembering and be ready to hit "record" when the time was right. It was by that simple mindset when I began to look at life differently.

What I learned was to be attentive and observant. When I look at my own life, I see a few similarities. If you're like me, you can get into a rut of living each day without really observing or mentally recording what's going on around you and in you. Life tends to feel mundane and familiar if we're not careful to fight against it. Following this family's story taught me to continually anticipate meaningful and exciting things to happen around me and to be ready to engage with them.

If you're willing to look, there are people in your life right now who simply need to hear, "You're loved, and you're worth it." Sometimes those people are in your own home, and other times they're complete strangers. God calls us to seek out and love not only those who we want but also those who are broken and keep love at an arm's length. Life is full of opportunities to love people. We just have to be intentional at times to notice them.

I sometimes look back to Little Katya's story and see my relationship with God in it. I can picture all the people and experiences the Lord has put in my life and see how the evil in the world tempts me to say "no" to Him. He offers me, and you, an eternal home where we are loved and cared for. All we have to do is simply say, "yes." Too often, I'm left listening to the voices of evil. These are the voices who want to keep me locked into an existence that leads to misery and longing.

God pursues us, just like this family pursued Little Katya. Despite all of the kicking and screaming and crying, God patiently waits and bends down to quietly say, "I love you, you are mine, and I will pursue you." Even over a decade later, I'm thankful God provided such a clear and tangible representation of His love to me. I don't know where Little Katya or Little Ivan would be today if she had insisted on staying in Ukraine, but I do know the next time my prized possession better suits someone else's needs, it's theirs without hesitation.

Vanishing Cats

God says He will never give us more than we can handle, but sometimes I think He moves us to the brink so we look towards Him.

For most of my adventure in Ukraine, the people I hung out with gathered at a Chinese restaurant in Lugansk each week for church. Each Sunday morning, several of us loaded up the car and drove the hour's drive to the city. The commute was more like a long bus route than a casual drive to church. We often made several stops in neighboring villages to pick up people who wanted to go to church with us. Some of the people we picked up were strange, some stinky, and others loud.

We didn't care who you were as long as you'd get in the car with us. Our car removed the ability to keep someone at an arm's distance, which was exciting and uncomfortable. It was always a refreshing time to be in the car with people I cared about and people I thought were a little strange. It was an opportunity to catch up on life and enjoy each other's company, even if it looked like a clown car as a seemingly endless stream of people piled out when we finally made it to church.

I looked forward to Sundays because it was a time to meet with people I didn't get to see throughout the week. Plus, we almost always went out to eat pizza after church, and I looked forward to that. It didn't matter that I didn't understand every word of the songs we sang or of the sermon we heard; I was around people who were reaching out to Jesus. They always gave me the sense He was reaching back.

Authentic Chinese immigrants ran the Chinese restaurant we met in for church. From my point of view, their bodies were in Ukraine, but their hearts were in a distant land. It seemed they had a close-knit community together, and they rarely ventured beyond their group. They were in Ukraine looking for a better life than what they had in their homeland, and owning a restaurant in the eastern part of the country allowed them the opportunity.

I enjoyed observing Jing, the man who immigrated from China and lived in the same village as me, interacting with the restaurant owners. His story was like theirs. More than a decade before I met Jing, he dropped everything in China and moved to Lugansk. He too was looking for more opportunity and a better life. I could tell by watching Jing and the restaurant owners interact that it was refreshing for them to speak Chinese together and share a distant culture that felt like home. I understood this connection because I too was refreshed by other Americans who shared my language and culture.

Jing chose to follow Christ years before I met him. In fact, Adam had been the one to share Jesus with him. He was a farmer in the village I lived in before walking with the Lord. As his heart changed, so did his entire life's mission. He became a full-time minister to the growing Chinese community in Lugansk and intensely loved his family and neighbors.

It was always a joy to watch Jing translate the sermon into Chinese for the restaurant owners. I couldn't understand the sermon any better than the restaurant owners, and I certainly didn't understand Chinese, so I watched Jing as he faithfully communicated with people who shared his geographic origins. It was sometimes painful to watch the loving frustration Jing experienced as it seemed he made slow, if any, progress with the owners. The smile and jovial spirit Jing seemed always to have was contagious, but the restaurant owners were resistant and skeptical.

The restaurant itself was not visible from the road. In fact, it wasn't exactly visible even if you knew what you were looking for. I second-guessed myself the first time I arrived at the restaurant's doors. There was no sign or any identifying attributes for the establishment, only a dark metal door in an alleyway. I'm fairly certain you couldn't have found this place by searching for it on Google Maps or Yelp.

The restaurant was buried in the basement of a four-story building so it could have the cheapest rent possible. Its only entrance was located in the dirt alley between the neighboring building. The main door opened to a staircase, which led down into a basement that had a slight smell of mildew. Each time the metal door closed, it seemed like the building shook and echoed. As you descended into the restaurant, the air became thick and damp, and the lights inside were dim. The place had more of a mafia feel than a church.

The restaurant owners loved our company because it was business for them even if they weren't sure about the whole Jesus thing. We never had more than 30 people in attendance at our church. Even at that number, the place was packed. Nobody was falling out in the Holy Spirit because there was nowhere to fall. It was the kind of place where everyone knew everybody, and if you missed a Sunday, all would know about it.

We didn't have Sunday School or any other alternative programming at church; it was simply a time for a body of people to gather to worship Jesus and enjoy each other's company. No fancy lights or big screens reflected what was happening on stage, and in most cases, we didn't even have a microphone. We each stood together as one singing familiar songs. In this Chinese restaurant, I first discovered church isn't a building; it's a body of people together worshiping Jesus.

Not only was the restaurant filled with all of us humans, but the restaurant owners also seemed to have no problem sharing their space with a few random cats. To be honest, I don't know if the cats belonged to the owners or if they were just cat people and didn't mind their company. Either way, it was fairly common to see a cat zoom by the stage in the middle of a church service as it let out a loud screech. I think we bothered them.

As time went on, more and more cats seemed to hang around the restaurant. I imagine word got out in the cat community that the restaurant always put out some food for them. By the time winter came, the cat population seemed to have multiplied by a few folds. I'm not suggesting the Chinese restaurant was dabbling in the cat rescue or breeding business, but they certainly weren't doing much to slow the procreation either. I think there were more cats inside and around the restaurant in the colder months than there were people.

For a while, I had a working theory that the cats were used from time to time as free protein for the restaurant owners when resources got scarce. Every once in a while, I'd notice the cat population get just a little smaller. It wouldn't be long until the cat gang was back up to full capacity, but I couldn't help but notice one or two going "missing" from time to time. It didn't seem others ever noticed the population swing, or maybe they too tried to ignore it. Regardless, it was an unspoken rule that we never talked about the evolving cat population. My observation haunted me from time to time, but I could usually skate by without eating at the restaurant after church, so I chose to keep my mouth shut.

Not everyone who attended church ate at the restaurant. Many people who attended church couldn't afford to eat at a restaurant, and others simply chose not to. A handful of churchgoers ate at the restaurant week after week, but the owners knew not all of us would eat at once. I usually opted for the pizza place around the corner; it seemed to be a safer option.

One week in particular, one of us had the idea to schedule a date where all of us at church would eat together at the restaurant after the service. Adam and I convinced everyone to let us cover their meal and pitched in for those who couldn't afford to eat out. We set a date for a few weeks in the future and then let the restaurant owners know about the plan we'd hatched. The owners were thrilled about our plans and acted as we had just given them a huge gift. To be honest, I don't know what they said in return as it was all in Chinese, and Jing was busy doing other things at the time. But, from the smiles on their faces and their hands around my cheeks, I'm reasonably sure they were good things. They were ecstatic, but even still, I was apprehensive about the deal. I remembered my theory about the cats, but I knew we were too far in on the deal to back out now.

A few weeks later, the Sunday came when we had planned our big feast. I became more nervous as time grew near. I still remembered my theory. As we approached the date, I kept a quiet and watchful eye on the restaurant's cat population. I didn't go as far as naming each cat; I feared it would be too risky emotionally. However, each one of them had an assigned number. I prayed the cats would run away or find a better home somewhere, but they seemed to absolutely love living around the Chinese restaurant.

On the morning of our planned feast, we got an extra early start making our rounds as a taxi service. Considering we had announced we'd be paying for the meals, we had a higher than typical attendance. The car we had could safely fit seven people inside, but we ended up with at least twelve that day. We spared no room and threw all safety precautions out of the window.

Laps became seats, and all understandings of personal space were null and void.

As usual, we bumped and bounced our way towards the Chinese restaurant in the city. I remembered my theory about the cats, and I prayed the entire way there that God would intervene. I even filled my pockets with cat treats with the hopes of drawing all nearby cats to me so I could get a headcount when I arrived. As we neared the restaurant, I began to think of creative outs I could claim if my fears had been proven correct.

My options grew thin, and I started to get desperate. I considered making this the Sunday I'd choose to do some street evangelism instead of attending actual church. I also considered becoming vegetarian. None of my options seemed like they'd hold water, so I decided to commit to whatever was ahead.

As we pulled up to the restaurant, I must have looked like a crazy person as I walked around the perimeter of the establishment trying to discreetly call any nearby cats to me. I quietly snapped and whistled, but I saw no signs of any cats around. It must have looked like I had suddenly developed Tourette Syndrome as I received awkward glances from the people around me. My fears started to grow louder in my head, and I felt sick to my stomach. As I looked around at the larger than normal church crowd, I didn't sense anyone else was acknowledging the unfortunate but increasingly obvious truth. The cats were nowhere to be found, and my hope was fading.

The church service went on as usual, although this time cats didn't worship with us. I'm fairly sure I prayed louder and more fervently that day, but I was careful not to make any overt pleas for the cats' return. I don't think I sang much that Sunday, and I definitely couldn't tell you what the sermon was about. Everyone seemed to carry on as usual, but I was freaking out in my mind. I had enough evidence now to reasonably believe there was some nefarious play involving the cats. Still, I knew I couldn't prove it. Maybe the restaurant owners knew they have more people in the restaurant that Sunday and made an effort to clear out the non-human life. I still doubt that alternative theory to this day, but it helps keep me sane.

As the church service ended, I knew my fate was sealed. We were all committed to staying for lunch after church, and it was obvious the restaurant owners were delighted to have a full house. As we all found our seats, the food began coming out in heaps. I couldn't help but picture the scene from Matilda involving the chocolate cake as I looked at the restaurant's owners. The whole thing felt sinister and dirty, but I didn't want to be rude.

The restaurant owners held nothing back, and they prepared the meal in a traditional Chinese way. I've never seen so much rice, vegetables, soup and, yes, meat. Piles of meat. We've all heard of "mystery meat" from our school or summer camp days, but this experience took the cake and icing. I gave glancing stares around the room to see if I was alone in my fears, but I didn't receive much in return from those around me. The restaurant owners pre-determined the portions, and each person received a plate piled high with everything they offered that day. Everyone simply began gorging on the feast as it arrived in front of them.

Not wanting to be the odd one out, and in an attempt to not offend our over-joyed hosts, I too began eating. Each chew caused a grimace and nervous anticipation, and I tried to hide my emotions from my face. My stomach turned with each bite, and I tried to quiet the audible groans it made. The restaurant owners stood around, smiling ear to ear in excited anticipation, similar to how my grandmother does at Thanksgiving. There was no chance of getting away with the polite chew then spit into a napkin. It was clear the expectation was for every guest to make what my family called a "happy plate" when I was growing up. No food was to be left behind.

All of us ate what was on our plate that day. Some went back for seconds and thirds, but I was overly content with just one serving. For some strange reason, my appetite just wasn't too big on this particular day. I remained unusually quiet and reserved for the rest of the day after eating at the Chinese restaurant. I figured I'd be violently ill in a short amount of time, and I second-guessed each stomach rumbling throughout the day. Thankfully, I never saw my lunch from that day again, but my mental wellness had been damaged.

I still don't know whether the cats were part of our meal that day, but I know I never saw cats around the Chinese restaurant ever again. It was never formally labeled a faux pas subject, but to this day, nobody who was in attendance at the Chinese restaurant has spoken a public word about it. I'm pretty sure I'm fine physically. The doctor tells me I have nothing to worry about. Still, I can't think about it for too long, or I start second-guessing his medical opinion.

More than anything, my comfort was tested that day in the Chinese restaurant. It wasn't long after our feast when the government shut down the Chinese restaurant. I don't know why it was shut down, but I have a few fears as to why. Ukrainian health restrictions are much lower than in America, and the restaurant still got shut down. Take that for what it's worth. Thankfully, we transferred our church to another nearby Chinese restaurant run by a different family. I never saw any cats around that place. All of our church members made it out alive, and now this story lives as a reminder to all of the Lord's provision and protection.

God knows our pressure points, and He knows how to push us. I think in some cases, the Lord presses into these points of contention in our life to help us grow. In other cases, God puts us in uncomfortable situations just to remind us of His promises. His Word says He will never give us more than we can handle, but sometimes I think He moves us to the brink so we look towards Him.

When I think of the mysteriously disappearing cats, I'm reminded that following Jesus isn't always easy. In fact, there are many times in my life when I question why God decided to allow a particular set of circumstances to happen. You have too, I bet. Sometimes, I find myself angry at God as I question His intentions, all the while knowing He could have orchestrated any set of events to take place. Every once in a while, it feels like Jesus is pushing me away, but in reality, He simply wants me to turn around and be reminded I need Him.

I sometimes look back to that day in the Chinese restaurant and wonder why God chose the one thing I was most uncomfortable with to test me. Maybe this was His way of making me grow or teaching me to rely on Him. I think it's easy to say I trust God when things are easy or seemingly normal. Things get a little more difficult when I'm stretched and unsure of what's going on around me. From my perspective, Jesus intentionally places obstacles in our path just to see us turn towards Him like a kid as we say, "I need help."

I'm not insinuating you need to eat cats to please God. In fact, please do not eat cats. That's likely bad for you. I think what pleases God is the trust we place in Him. Doing so requires us to think less of ourselves and more about God's character. When we put our fears down for just a second to allow God to lead us, we tend to grow. Strife and pain compete with growth. God knows this, and He looks at you and me both and reminds us He's enough for us to be triumphant.

If you're like me, times of growth will come at a cost. On that day in the Chinese restaurant, the price was a mental and emotional one for me. I knew what was likely going on, but I also knew God was in control. For you, your call to trust God may come at an even bigger and longer-lasting cost. What if He calls you to a dangerous part of the world? What if following Jesus means less time with your friends and family? What if your cost is forgoing the money and career you're capable of earning and trading it for a life of lesser means for the sake of others? All of these things are possible when following Jesus.

Wrapping my mind around the thought of abandoning all for the sake of following Christ is a difficult thing at times. I like being comfortable. You do too, and that's okay. What's important is our willingness to let go and to follow Him. God used that day in the Chinese restaurant, cats and all, to demonstrate a deeper level of trust that is possible in Him.

If you haven't heard, Jesus did some pretty wild things in the Bible involving food and trust, and I think He was making a strange modern rendition in my case. Jesus' disciples questioned His ability to feed a large crowd with only a small amount of food, but Jesus simply asked them to trust Him. He asked me to do just as His disciples did that day. The same God is alive today, and the same truths still exist as they did thousands of years ago. Jesus simply asks us to trust Him.

As you move forward in your walk with Jesus, always remember who is leading you. Earthly leaders often let us down. Everyone is a leader of someone, and I promise you, you've let your followers down at some point. The beautiful truth is God will never let us down. Sure, it may be painful at times. We may even question if it's really Him leading us from time to time. Our skepticism is a good thing. It means we're being analytical and careful about which direction we steer our lives in.

Compare every nudge you have against the Bible and see if what you're feeling inspired to do would be written in the pages of God's Word or not. Get real with God. Be honest with Him. Ask Him for strength and courage and trust His answers. The call to follow Jesus isn't promised to be an easy one. In fact, the Bible talks about counting the cost of following Him.

God made you the way you are for a reason. Rejoice in this. Know that God works for the good of His people and trust Him to lead you as you set out to serve Him. I promise you will encounter a few Chinese restaurants and cats along the way, but continue to look up towards Jesus and know His way is better than yours. He won't let you down.

Mr. Tony

Some people talk about doing and some people just do. I want to be the kind of person who simply does.

I wish I didn't have to tell you this, but Mr. Tony is dead. In fact, Mr. Tony died several years ago. He was an older man from Louisiana with an accent to prove it. His past was pretty troubled. According to Mr. Tony, he was a hardcore alcoholic back in his day. He wasn't the kind of guy who occasionally drank too much in hopes of having a good time. He habitually went all out when it came to the bottle. According to him, he'd come home on Friday after a long week of work and settle into his couch with a gallon of vodka and make it disappear before Monday morning. He'd also reserve a six-pack of beer to "sober" him on the way to work Monday morning, you know, just to get over his hangover. At his worse, it's safe to say Mr. Tony drank to stay alive, not for enjoyment.

His belly full of booze was often accompanied by a cigarette hanging from a mouth fit for a sailor based upon his accord. Although I never heard him use foul language, I took him at his word that he knew how to throw a few four-letter utterances around. It's hard to tell how many years he lived this way because I'm not certain even Mr. Tony knew. He seemed to remember his past in only fuzzy details and in a disorganized timeline.

It was difficult for me to imagine the version of Mr. Tony that he recounted, because the Mr. Tony I knew was one of the nicest people I've ever met. There was something about him that just seemed to shine. I don't mean in a fake way, the way some people smile and exchange pleasantries with you but secretly gossip about every person they've ever encountered. Mr. Tony was genuine, and it's something I immediately understood when I met him.

During the short time I knew Mr. Tony, I often wondered why he was always so happy and cheerful. After all, he told me he never married and had only his brother left in his life. Everyone else had already died. He was the kind of man who seemed to have a glass half full, even if he occasionally stumbled and spilled a little out.

One day in late fall, Mr. Tony showed up at the house where I lived in the village. To be clear, he had been invited, but nobody talked much about him coming to Ukraine until he arrived. He just kind of appeared one day. I didn't have much of a gauge to predict why Mr. Tony was traveling from Louisiana to Ukraine. When I met him, he told me he was staying for a month. In fact, he was going to be my roommate.

I learned a call had been put out for people to come to Ukraine to help repair the camp and prepare it for the next summer. There were leaky pipes, banged-up walls and doors, and other jobs fit for a handyman as with any old facility. I guess Mr. Tony felt up to the job, although I don't think he was particularly qualified for any task in particular. He arrived with no ambition of a vacation or even a sense of adventure. He seemed to be content with rolling his sleeves up and simply working, and that's what he was in Ukraine to do.

Traveling such a distance was not in the interest of someone of his age or health, but Mr. Tony had a determined spirit. I can only imagine what the last leg of the flight into Ukraine must have looked like. The small plane was likely full of locals who spoke Russian and fit into certain cultural norms, and then there was Mr. Tony. He didn't speak a lick of Russian, and even if a Ukrainian on the plane knew some English, they likely didn't understand Mr. Tony's brand of deep-south Louisiana English. Regardless, I was happy to have another person I could sit and speak fluently with while in Ukraine. I needed someone else to share stories with, even if I needed a translator for some of Mr. Tony's southern phrases.

The beauty of Mr. Tony is there is nothing remarkable about his life in terms of earthly achievements. He wasn't a high-powered lawyer or doctor, he wasn't a successful business-man, and he never even had a family of his own. If anything, Mr. Tony had lived a relatively rough life until a few years before our introduction. What he did have was the love of Christ and a story of redemption, and that was more than enough for him. It seemed each day was a reminder of the second chance the Lord had given him. Each morning the sun came up, so did he with a smile on his face and a heart facing outward.

Mr. Tony always wore tennis shoes, light-colored blue jeans, and a faded button-up plaid shirt. He presented himself as he saw himself, a simple, southern man who had nothing to prove. His face was cleanly shaven each morning, and he never wore a hat despite his thin gray hair. He was horizontally challenged but was also a tall man. Mr. Tony didn't seem much concerned with the way others viewed his physical appearance. It struck me that he was far more interested in portraying what was inside him. He didn't mind you having to fight past his outward appearance to discover what he was about.

For the brief time I knew Mr. Tony, we spent each of our

days primarily working at the camp in our village. Each day offered a new task, but none of them promised any public recognition or even simple gratitude. We rose early each morning, often before the sun, to get a quick breakfast in us, and then it was off to work. We could walk to camp from Adam's house, so we traced our steps to and from camp each day.

Each morning's walk was down the same dusty and empty village streets. We'd walk past neighboring village homes, the small village store which wasn't yet open, and a creek that ran the distance of the road. Most mornings, we'd encounter the village cow chained up awaiting its owner. The cow greeted us each morning with a loud "moo" but didn't seem all too interested in interacting further with us.

The conversations we held while in transit usually consisted of brief recaps of the day before and what we hoped for in the day ahead. There was nothing groundbreaking or overly important discussed during our short morning meetings. Still, our conversations were a chance to wake up and share a few words with the person you were bound to spend all day working beside. Once we arrived at camp after our short walk each morning, it was time to work. The talking was mostly over until we repeated our morning's steps in reverse back to Adam's house.

After each day of work, Mr. Tony would sit around with Adam's family and me and share whatever was on his mind. He didn't seem to have a pre-formulated agenda or any talking points, he simply wanted to spend time with the people around him. From my perspective, he wasn't used to having someone to spend his evenings with, but he seemed to enjoy our company. Often, Mr. Tony would share stories about his days before knowing Christ and remind us of the redemption in his life.

His struggle with the bottle he grasped for so many years still lived in his head. He allowed recounts of his past to infiltrate conversations, but I don't believe he did it intentionally. It's almost as if he placed all the shortcomings of his life inside the bottle he once held and allowed it to carry the burden and shame of his former self. Regardless of his tendency to interrupt, he seemed to have a genuine interest in engaging with those around him. Mr. Tony didn't seem to put a silver lining on his life. He simply wanted to engage with you and share the good, the bad, and the ugly. In his mind, your story was just as important as his, maybe even more so.

He wasn't shy about showing us a growth he had on his belly. I think he used this abnormality to demonstrate a profound change in him. The growth was opposite of his heart, just below his rib cage. He told us the lump was due to health issues he developed back in his drinking days, but he never gave specifics. Mr. Tony's doctors seemed fixated on Mr. Tony's abnormality based on the pills they sent with him to Ukraine. As he'd tell you, most of the medications he took had some effect or interaction with the growth on his upper stomach. He didn't purposely display the large bump under his shirt, but he didn't try to hide it either. It was both a curse of his past and a reminder of hope for his future.

I could undoubtedly see Mr. Tony was not in the best health, evidenced by the collection of pill bottles his doctor sent with him on his trip, but his spirit was always glowing. Night after night, Mr. Tony took a multitude of doctor-prescribed pills in a ritualistic way. He never complained, nor seemed bothered, that another person observed him as he did this. It seemed to be too intrinsically intertwined with his existence for it to matter to him. Each night, Mr. Tony would separate his pills on the kitchen table, organizing them in a way I didn't understand. He would methodically take each one with a swig of water and then double-check to make sure he hadn't forgotten one. It seemed as if the pills allowed his body to get by, but God made his spirit flourish.

I have to imagine each pill was a painful reminder of his previous life, but also a stark reminder of the power of Christ. Each swallow of a pill seemed to be met with a flashback of prior mistakes. Maybe Mr. Tony viewed every little detail of his current life as a reminder that God was sustaining his every day and every movement. He seemed thankful each morning to have another chance at living life aimed at glorifying Christ. Each pill was a catalyst for realizing his future hopes and dreams, even as an old man.

During his stay, Mr. Tony and I shared a room. Our room was simple. It had only two twin beds in it and a window that looked towards the back yard of Adam's house. The same river which flowed parallel to the path we walked to camp each morning could be seen from our bedroom window. I fit on my twin bed slightly better than Mr. Tony fit on his, but he never complained. In fact, I don't ever remember hearing Mr. Tony complain about anything.

He went to bed before I did and was up before me too. For him, the sun and moon were better indicators of when one should sleep. He always left the light on for me at night and never turned it on before I was up. He was kind and thoughtful, but I felt bad for him sleeping with the light shining. He insisted on keeping it on no matter what I said.

Mr. Tony never drew attention to himself and seemed to always think of others first. It was an admirable trait. The longer I was around him, the more I realized how unimportant being noticed was to him. He was content living life in the shadows; he might have even preferred it. I like to think Mr. Tony had a silent contract with Jesus to simply be ready when he was needed, nothing more. It was almost like Mr. Tony lived on stand-by with a phone in his hand. You wouldn't know he had been called to help you, but given the chance, Mr. Tony would be by your side ready to get to work. The task didn't matter as long as he contributed to a better outcome for you and the mission you were on.

While Mr. Tony was in Ukraine, he was a brief member of Team Hot Water. I introduced you to this elite team a few chapters ago. I'm sure Mr. Tony had no idea he'd be swinging an axe while he was in Ukraine, but it didn't seem to bother him. As far as I could tell, he moved a little slower than the younger crowd, but I suppose that was due to his age, not just his toxic past. After all, Mr. Tony was at least three times my age, even with a conservative estimate.

Even though he visited when we didn't have hundreds of kids running around, we still had various people staying at the camp and wanted to give them hot water for their showers. We prided ourselves on providing excellent care to whoever stayed at our camp. The fact there weren't any kids present didn't mean we could slack in our duties. Whether you were an orphan kid living at our camp for two weeks or a Ukrainian militia member doing military training in our camp's off-season, Team Hot Water wanted you to feel catered to.

The physical labor took more from Mr. Tony's aging body than it did mine, but he never mentioned it. As I watched him work, I never saw him take the back seat. He always seemed to be the first to begin and the last to-finish a task. He was humble enough to take a quick water break, but he was careful never to let his momentary recharge present itself as laziness.

Work seemed to be the constant for Mr. Tony; it was his catalyst to pour into people. The example he set was quiet yet powerful. He didn't look around to see who was watching, and he didn't appear to even want gratitude from those he worked for. He was straightforward in his approach; just be present and do what was asked of him. If you asked Mr. Tony to get a job done, you could consider it done before he even started.

Time spent working around Mr. Tony grew to be a valuable lesson. I began to understand obedience in God's calling doesn't mean there's always some glorious display or revelation of God's plan. Sometimes answering God's call is just a simple and quiet obedience to where He has called you. If you're like me, you sometimes fall into the trap that following Christ to other nations, your office or school, or even in your own home has to have fireworks or hands lifted high for it to be real. As I've learned, more often than not, following Christ takes the form of quiet obedience. My experiences have shown me that being obedient to God's calling often means knowing there's a silent contract between my Creator and me. My role is to pursue my end of the bargain, following Him faithfully.

I wish more than anything I could tell Mr. Tony how much of an impact he had on me. He probably had no idea. He helped teach me I don't have to be fancy or a Christian superstar to be obedient to Christ. Mr. Tony understood when Christ calls you to do something, you just go. You don't need a special talent or groundbreaking idea. You simply need to answer the phone when God calls.

I like to believe Mr. Tony was met at the gates of Heaven with a hug from Jesus when he passed. He lived a rough life for most of his existence, and I imagine meeting Jesus was a welcomed relief from his struggles. If you've read through the Bible, you may recall a part where God talks about welcoming a good and faithful servant. I have to imagine God knew Mr. Tony's name when He thought up that part of His Word.

I know when I get to Heaven, I'm going to find Mr. Tony and give him the hug I never got to give him on earth. He taught me that in life, and in God's calling, you just have to go. There won't always be fireworks or parades when you follow Jesus. It may just be you, Jesus, and the people you are interacting with. That's alright. Jesus is enough, and those fancy displays of radical Christianity don't mean a whole lot if you try to outshine Christ.

Mr. Tony's life reminds me God doesn't judge us by our achievements or accolades. He judges us by our hearts. Mr. Tony's heart was pure, and it made me want to love Christ more. I don't know about you, but when the day comes that I pass on, I hope someone can say the same about my heart. If that happens to be the case, I can safely say I've lived a life worth living as a faithful servant of the Lord.

New Wallpaper

You don't have to change the world to change somebody's world.

People who know me well can attest to the fact that I am a self-diagnosed germaphobe. I've been called Dr. Pressley several times in my life because I look like a surgeon preparing for surgery when it comes time to eat. In fact, my knuckles sometimes crack and bleed because I wash my hands so often and so thoroughly. I've long dealt with the awkward glances in public restrooms as eager hand washers look at me with amazement and the wish that I'd hurry up. I've seen more than a few people's patience run out and leave without hitting the soap and water.

Through the years, I've learned to join in on the joking. Because after all, if you are going to have hands that look like an alligator's back, you better learn to roll with the punches. I'm not sure exactly sure where my obsession with washing my hands came from, but I do know God must have a sense of humor. I told you about a few disappearing cats a few chapters ago, but God wasn't done drawing me out of my comfort zone yet.

There were several other villages tucked away down dusty dirt roads between my village and the closest city. They were much like the one I lived in. When driving from my village to the city, vast fields of sunflowers next to impoverished villages filled with pain and longing reminded me of God's beauty among human suffering. My mind automatically categorized the scene as the difference between what is God-given and what is man-made. It was difficult to drive and not consider the hardships of the village people. I saw it in my village too, but the continuous reminder during the hour drive to the city seemed to leave a lasting impression in my mind. It was like watching a slideshow, only each slide depicted the same misery and disappointment as the one before.

I often wrestled with where to start in helping the people I saw. There seemed to be too many problems, and too few resources to accomplish anything meaningful. Choosing where to start could have been as easy as throwing a rock in any direction and getting to work wherever it landed. Once the work was done, I could have aimlessly thrown the rock again and started the whole process over. I often felt tired when thinking of who and how to help. My outlook seemed to swing from depressing helplessness to radiant excitement that there was work to be done, and I was there to do it.

One day, I received word from one of our local interpreters and ministry partners that a single mother lived in one of the villages I often passed. The mother's name was Anna, and there was no father in the family's picture. This lady had several young kids and no real way to provide for them, but it seemed she did what she could to meet their needs. Anna didn't seem to be neglectful, but her situation was dire, and she needed a helping hand.

A few of us decided to stop by one day, but I'm not sure any of us knew what to expect or what we'd like to do for this mother. We quickly found out this woman wasn't an ordinary woman. In fact, we learned she was a prostitute, and the home she shared with her kids was her office. She had seven children, but only five lived in her house with her. One was in an orphanage, the other was sick in the hospital, and neither got to see their mother. Of the five kids who lived in her home, all were covered in grime and clearly were not getting enough nutrition. It was evident Anna struggled to provide for her family and didn't hold herself in high esteem. Her situation broke my heart.

Anna had trouble looking anyone in the eye. I sensed her problems were equally rooted in shame and deceit. I can't pretend I understand what it must feel like to be in her situation, but I wanted her to feel compassion and love. I'm not sure how long she had been living her lifestyle, but Anna seemed beat down and tired. By looking at her, I could tell she sensed her walls were closing in and hope of a positive outcome was an increasingly fleeting possibility.

Anna and her family lived in a house that consisted of a few rooms neglected of sanitation or organization. The house, like most in the villages, was small and in disrepair. There was no running water, and the doors and windows didn't close properly. In the summer, flies entered and exited as they pleased, as did the snow in the winter.

Inside the home, Anna's babies were not forced to wear diapers, so traces of human urine and feces were scattered around the house. The whole family slept on one mattress, located on the ground in the middle of the main room. There were no sheets or pillows on the bed; it was simply a dingy mattress. It was beyond filthy and was big enough for two adults. Given Anna's unfortunate line of work, it was likely shared by more than just the family, if you get my drift.

There were piles of dirty clothes lying around and stacks of dirty dishes lying next to buckets of water that had a brown tint. Flies filled the air as well as an accompanying stench too foul to parse out. Outside, Anna's kids ran around with faces and clothes so ground in with filth that it would take a little more than just water to cleanse. I was so far out of my comfort zone that I needed a map to get back.

When I met Anna, I understood her problems would become generational, and I wanted so badly for her kids to know a different way of life. Anna's children faced a grim battle for self-worth and confidence in their current state, and I didn't want them to repeat their mother's mistakes. I wasn't naive enough to believe I had any power to simply walk in and change Anna's life, but I knew I could start chipping away at the boulder in front of me. It was sure to be a difficult task, but the effort seemed inevitable and necessary.

I asked God why He had chosen me to help Anna's family. Nonetheless, I felt deep down, helping Anna and her kids was what Jesus would have done if He had walked by. It was no mistake that God had led me to Anna's house, but internally, I was combative with the idea of helping her. The conditions were beyond terrible and I, as well as most others, had a genuine fear for their health, and ours, as we worked in Anna's house. It would have been best to burn the place down and rebuild it, but that was clearly not going to happen given the resources at our disposal.

It wasn't Anna or her kids that got to me. God adored them, and I understood their infinite worth to Him. I saw the people in front of me as God's treasure, just like the sunflower fields that surrounded their house, and their home as a byproduct of the lack of confidence and value Anna saw in herself. Although I cared deeply for Anna's family, the house side of the issue was like a heat-seeking missile aimed at the core of my human fear and discomfort. I could almost hear Jesus saying, "I love *all* people, and you will too if you are going to follow me."

It shamed me to have second thoughts about helping these poor kids and their mother. I mean, who am I to wince at less than perfect conditions? After all, I hadn't moved to Ukraine to go on a fancy vacation; I was there to get down on my hands and knees and get dirty. If you read the Bible, you'll find several instances of Jesus *and* His followers choosing to spend time with the low and needy. I don't think Jesus meant for that mentality to expire.

If you're like me, some of your major life changes probably started with someone merely taking the time to be with you and to pour a little of themselves into you. There are rare times in my life I can recount when there was an explosive and immediate change in my life's circumstances or personal standing. For me, change seems to start slowly and quietly, often out of love from someone looking at my life from their perspective. For Anna, I knew she needed someone to say, "I see you, and I believe in you," and that's what I wanted to accomplish.

After officially deciding Anna's family was our next engagement, we devised a plan of action. We chose to discuss our plans outside the home because, frankly, being inside the house for too long was accompanied by a gag reflex and the invasive desire to forget about the whole project. Standing in a small circle, we started throwing out ideas of ways we could help. We obviously needed to help solve the food and water situation for the kids, but we also wanted to do something more, which would leave a visual reminder of a possible new beginning for Anna.

As we tossed around ideas, one of our partners mentioned cleaning the walls and putting up new wallpaper. In my mind, the idea was a little short-sighted because I gravitated towards cleaning up the bucket filled with human feces sitting on the counter before I could think about new wallpaper. In my mind, the problems Anna faced were larger than how her walls looked, but I was approaching the issue from a different angle than those around me.

After a few minutes, it was apparent wallpaper was the

direction the group was headed in, so I agreed with a puzzled look on my face. After all, new wallpaper was a step closer to a civilized home for this family, so I figured it couldn't hurt. With our plan finalized, we asked one of our female partners to take Anna into town to buy a few groceries while we worked. Once Anna was out of sight, we began working with a purpose. It must have looked like we were on one of those home renovation shows on HGTV the way we were ripping things apart.

We didn't have a lot of time or materials, so we kept our work simple but hopefully effective. My arms spent a lot of time stretched as far from my face and body as they would allow as I carefully removed human waste and soiled materials. We did our best to clean surfaces with the strongest cleaning agent we could find. We mopped the floor and organized the home the best we could. I would have paid an unreasonable amount of money for latex gloves and a respirator that day.

After a few hours, we had finished the task. The old wallpaper had been torn down, and the new stuff was put up. While the place certainly looked better, you still wouldn't find this project on a Pinterest board and be overly excited or eager to try it yourself. My outlook on merely changing the wallpaper and tidying up hadn't changed a whole lot from when we started.

Regardless of my opinion, the home looked far better off when we finished than when we started, but it wasn't perfect. After several hours, Anna returned to her house in tears, amazed and thankful for the work we'd done. Seeing her face made the entire project, and all its pitfalls, worth it. There was almost nothing we did to Anna's home that she couldn't have done herself, but I have to imagine her situation didn't lend itself to a high value of self-worth or belief that she could make positive changes herself.

When I think of Anna, I think of myself and the problems I have. We all have things in our lives that we know need some changes. If others walked through our lives, they too would see a few grimy spots. Some areas of my life have been historically shameful, and God continues to work in my story. I'm sure if you and I sat down for a talk, you could share some areas of your life that are just the same. It's human nature, but I think God made us like this on purpose. He delights in walking alongside us, helping us make changes, and setting our sights on better futures. We aren't meant to be stagnant in our growth, but sometimes we get set in our ways and need a push.

Shame is a dirty thing, and we too often allow it to put up barriers in our lives. Sometimes, we just need someone to come in and say, "I see your struggle, and I still love you." We too often choose not to ask for help or confide in those we trust because we are afraid of what others will think. Like Anna, we look at our lives' dirty walls and know there's a better way but choose to allow shame to overrule what we know needs changing.

From time to time, we all choose to live in our filth instead of trying to clean things up. For me, it often feels like others pointing their fingers at me in judgment, but in reality, it's my shame and guilt abusing my soul that prevents me from initiating change in my life. At the core of it, it's an irrational way of living, but sin in our lives tries desperately to prevent progress towards healing. The glimmers of hope and love in our lives are smothered when we give sin a louder voice than Jesus. In my experience, it's not until I surrender myself to uncomfortable conversations with those who love me, including Jesus, that I can progress down the road of redemption.

The truth is, God doesn't seem to put us in our comfort zone when He wants to teach us something. It's rarely the good times in my life when I feel a course correction from God. I usually screw something up or hurt someone else before I can feel Jesus pulling me towards Him. I think God designed us that way on purpose. We all struggle with wanting to feel like we're in control, but sometimes what we really need is someone stepping in with a helping hand extended to help us steer our ship.

When I study God's Word, I don't see Jesus taking a hands-off approach in the lives around Him. I more often see Jesus jumping in and getting His hands dirty for the sake of pointing people towards Him. It's not until I give up my comfort, pride, and know-it-all attitude that I'm able to invite Jesus into the lion's den of my problems as we combat them together. That's when I sense Jesus the most as He walks beside me, saying, "I'm enough."

As I stood with Anna and her kids, I couldn't help but think we just put a polishing touch on a much deeper problem in her life. Even with how much I want to believe the opposite, it is most likely true our efforts that day didn't radically change Anna's life for the long-term. I think, at best, God allowed us to shine a beam of light into Anna's life. Maybe that light still glimmers from time to time, like sunlight through the branches of a big tree on a sunny day. I hope the whispers of love we spoke to Anna eventually become triumphant shouts of joy as her heart bends towards the redeeming grace and mercy found in Jesus.

I have to imagine the new wallpaper was not very helpful in the grand scheme of Anna's needs, but God knew that going into it. God knew you don't have to change *the* world to change *somebody's* world. He also knew if I picked up a rock and hit Anna's house or some other random person's house that day, He was going to be behind our efforts the entire way. New wallpaper didn't solve Anna's poverty, and it didn't ensure her kids would be well fed or have a bright future, but it did something for her soul, which is worthwhile.

Sure, we gave Anna some new wallpaper and cleaned her place up a bit, but our image—our walls—don't have to be pretty for Jesus to love us. What God sees when He looks at you and me is far different than how we see our reflection in a mirror. God remembers each man and woman is made in His image, and he still sees the beauty and semblance of His majesty when He looks towards us. Despite our filth and problems, Jesus looks at you and me and smiles. When the mirrors of our lives get so dingy that we can't see an accurate picture of ourselves, Jesus stands behind us and whispers, "You're loved." He sees the past and present mess in our lives and still loves us, no matter our shame or guilt.

I have to imagine confusion was going through Anna's mind when strangers showed up at her house to simply clean her home and put up new wallpaper. I'm sure she was equally skeptical and baffled. I still wonder if our short time with Anna had a lasting impact on her. I don't know what her circumstances are today, but I pray the name "Jesus" has a rich and redeeming sound to her now.

From time to time, I think of Anna, and I am reminded of God's love for all of us. He knew Anna's name just like He knew mine when I knocked on her door. Over and over, Jesus bends down to you and me and brushes us off as He reminds us of our eternal worth to Him. I still carry my germophobic habits with me, but Anna now provides a reminder every time I wash my hands. Because of her, I now know God loves me even when things are messy and dirty. God doesn't require me to be clean to approach Him. He simply says, "Here, take my hand."

Hospital Escapes and Private Jets
I used to think God didn't speak. I now hear Him saying, "I love you. Just trust me."

During my stay with the family who was adopting a handful of kids from Ukraine, I had the privilege of observing the behind-the-scene dynamics of a growing family. Just like my family or yours, there were times of joy, confusion, frustration, and utter chaos. Adding several kids at once to a family is a stressful and daunting task, not to mention doing it in a foreign country. When you add the fact the kids joining the family didn't yet speak your language, share your customs, and came from abusive and negligent backgrounds, you're bound to experience some discomfort. During my stay with the adopting family, these dynamics were present, and I had the privilege of calling the living room couch my bedroom and my ticket to the show.

From my vantage point, I had the opportunity to witness a variety of emotions. At some points, I questioned whether it was understood I was in the room observing the conversations taking place. It seemed tears, shouts, and smiles bounced around the room, sometimes almost simultaneously. Through the expressed doubt, fear, and sheer confusion of what was going on around them, the family I lived with offered various memorable moments for me to observe. We've all experienced moments of yelling, crying, door slamming, and regretful apologies that serve as bookends to each of our insensitivities and "me first" attitudes, and this family was no different. Most of the moments I could share with you are likely not too different than what you may have observed in your own home while growing up, but this story sent us into crisis mode.

As the adoption process neared its end, the coming commotion was unforeseen. Before the chaos began, we all spent our evening together, eating at a nearby restaurant, and having a relatively easy-going time. As the evening drew to a close, we all walked back to our apartment and settled down for the night. The family all piled into their respective, yet shared, rooms, and I took my place on the living room couch. As we turned the lights out and tucked in under our blankets, the apartment was quiet and calm. I fell asleep quickly as I was comfortable and tired from the day.

After several hours of uninterrupted sleep, I was startled awake by an intense screaming coming from the living room floor. My first thought in my jolted consciousness was someone must have certainly intruded into our apartment. After all, the family I was living with was attempting to adopt several kids from a nearby orphanage, and many locals didn't look upon that favorably. It was obvious a bunch of Americans lived in our apartment, and we wouldn't have been difficult to spot or track down as we frequently walked around outside during the day.

As I quickly wiped my eyes and threw the blanket draped around me to the ground, I realized we weren't being invaded. I sat up straight on the edge of the couch and focused my tired eyes on what was before me. Instead of an intruder, Robert, the father of the family, was on the floor, rolling in pain as tears rolled down his cheeks. I was equally confused and intrigued about what was happening before me.

Robert is a tall man and one who doesn't show a lot of outward emotion. He is a businessman, and his intellect outweighs his emotion at times. His personality certainly doesn't lend itself to practical jokes; Robert is too serious and reserved for that. One thing was for sure, he hadn't randomly decided to play a joke. This was for real.

As Robert rolled in pain on the ground, he made unintelligible groans and hopeful gasps for relief as he clutched his abdomen. He gave short yet piercing glances my way as he searched for some sense of someone coming to his aid. My mind lagged a few seconds as I processed his pleas for help before I jumped up and awkwardly approached him, not knowing where to place my hands. Even with no medical background, it was clear to me that Robert was suffering from some ailment in his stomach area, but I had no clue how to help.

In my quick assessment of the situation, I gathered it wasn't Robert's heart that was failing, so I felt some sense of comfort. My next thought was he must be suffering from food poisoning from the local restaurant we all dined at just a few hours before, but his pain seemed to be too great for anything related to a bad burger or chicken breast. After a few minutes of Robert rolling on the floor and me trying to recall all the episodes of *House* I'd seen, his wife, Victoria, frantically appeared in the living room. She, too, was tired and had been hurriedly woken from her sleep, and we were equally confused as to what was happening. For a moment, I was relieved that she had arrived to help her husband, but I quickly realized she and I both were equally clueless about how to help Robert.

Everyone handles stress and confusion differently. Some of us get quiet as I do, and others begin babbling or frantically moving around. Unfortunately, Victoria handles stress by laughing. I don't mean a quiet chuckle or two. She exhibited more of an outright fit of laughter. Before it was all said and done, she was on the ground, too, only she was rolling in laughter and confusion as her husband anguished in pain. I felt bad for Robert. He was clearly in a lot of pain with no relief in his immediate future, and his wife was lying beside him, laughing and repeating, "Oh, come on, what's wrong with you?" After several minutes of this bizarre situation, Victoria gathered herself enough to realize Robert needed proper medical attention.

By this point, the entire family was now in the living room. It looked like we were playing a bad game of charades as we all made choppy and uncertain movements towards Robert. We'd all retreat from Robert just as quickly as we had approached him. Fear and confusion were setting in and paralyzing our efforts to help him.

Unfortunately, I was on the older end of the kids in the apartment, and one of the two adults was rolling in pain on the floor. At this point in the family's adoption process, the orphanage allowed the kids to stay with their new parents and I felt some sense of duty to help calm the frantic children. But, I had no idea what was going on, much less how to explain it in Russian to them. My attempts to calm the situation by telling them everything was alright were met with frightful cries and panic. I can't blame them because I didn't believe what I was telling them any more than they did.

Being in a foreign country provided uncertain medical options for Robert. We didn't know what the number was for an ambulance, or even if Ukraine had an ambulance service, and we certainly didn't know where the closest hospital was. None of our phones had the capability of Google Maps, so our situation left us with the next best option: go the streets in the middle of the night and scream until we found someone who could help us. Even in the chaos of the night, this didn't seem like our brightest or most trustworthy idea. Nonetheless, we quickly agreed we didn't have better ideas and abandoned Robert on the living room floor to search for help.

After abandoning Robert, we all rushed into the streets below our apartment and began waving down anyone we could see. Given it was three o'clock in the morning, I'm sure most everyone thought we were crazy, on drugs, or entirely out of our minds. Random lights began to flick on in neighboring apartments above us, and old ladies came to the windows as they tightened their robes and adjusted their eyeglasses. They must have thought we were crazy, and I'm sure the Ukrainian police were soon to be hot on our trail.

After a few minutes of arm flailing and screaming, we defaulted to blocking the travel of a passing motorist and demanded they stop and speak with us. We knew our desperate attempts for help could be misconstrued as grand theft auto, but we didn't care. In our broken Russian, we collectively conveyed the state of our medical emergency to the passerby. With reluctant willfulness and threat of a car-jacking extinguished, the man in the car drew us a crude map of how to get to the nearest hospital.

By this point in my adventure in Ukraine, I was well adept in saying "Sorry," "Thank you," and "You're welcome" in Russian. In the moment, I forgot which phrase meant "Thank you," so I said all three with excitement and enthusiasm fit for a triumphant sporting event. With our only hope in hand, we sprinted back to the apartment and scooped Robert into our rented van to whisk him away to the nearest hospital. Hope was now in sight, even if it flickered in the distance.

Looking back, I don't remember who occupied the driver's seat on the way to the hospital. I have to imagine it was Victoria, but I think she had finally realized the seriousness of the situation for Robert and was tending to him in the back of the van. Regardless of who was behind the wheel, none of us had a valid license, and only a couple of us could have seen over the dash. If I drove us, it was a total blackout in my memory, so don't come asking questions if you're a part of the Ukrainian government. However, if you haven't found them by now, we knocked over a few road signs, which might need to be repaired.

As our brakes squealed to a halt in the proposed hospital parking lot, our hopes of medical rescue shrunk. Like most buildings in Ukraine, the hospital was unsuspecting and drab in appearance. If you're like me, you picture hospitals as somewhat modern with a big red cross stamped across the front of the building. I think we design hospitals like this in America to instill hope in the event you have to visit one. That wasn't the case for this particular building as it may as well have been an insurance firm or bank.

With all of our hopes tied up in the building before us actually being a hospital filled with knowledgeable doctors willing to take on a new case, we rushed Robert through the front doors. To our surprise, there was nobody in the lobby ready to take in ailing patients. Instead, a disinterested receptionist working the night shift met us. As I remember it, she was doodling on a notepad in front of her while smacking bubble gum. Instead of springing into action for our ailing patient, she mumbled something to the effect of, "What are you doing here?" In fairness, our disappointment may have been due to a gross miscalculation of expectations.

Despite the lackluster response from the front desk, we decided to present Robert to the receptionist. She reluctantly agreed to take him further back into the hospital, but not before a loud pop of her bubble gum and a look of disgust on her face. After what felt like an eternity of awkward glances which communicated, "This is where you take over," Robert was reluctantly ushered back to a triage area fit for dying livestock.

A quick assessment of the area revealed a variety of

patients. Some had head bandages with blood soaking through; others seemed to be completely fine and seemingly on vacation. Dirty bottles of unknown liquids littered the window seals, and tables had open-capped needles and bloody rags strewn on them. It appeared the operating room, recovery area, and waiting room were all combined into one misery-stricken place. Of all the things unclear in my mind at the time, one thing was certain. This "hospital" was not the place to get adequate medical care. If we stayed, Robert might have gotten some relief from his medical issues, but it may have come at the cost of a severe infection or worse.

As Victoria also surveyed the conditions of this so-called hospital, it was clear her husband would not be receiving treatment from this place. Like an Olympic runner, she left the room we had been dumped into and was back at the nurse's station before I could ask where she was going. The hospital didn't have security, but guards would have been no match for Victoria. She didn't concern herself with polite requests to use the phone; she simply tore it from the desk and began frantically making calls back to America.

After several minutes and many shared glances of terror and concern, Victoria explained a private medical jet had been obtained for Robert to safely return to America for treatment. I don't believe price ever entered the conversation with Victoria. I'm not saying she didn't care, but at this stage of the night, she would have taken out a second mortgage to get Robert out of the situation he was in. Whether it was a private medical flight or a funeral, Robert and Victoria were bound to spend some cash on this night. Thankfully, they opted for the life-saving route instead of admitting defeat.

The decision to evacuate Robert had been made. All we had to do was get him safely back to our van and to the nearest airport to await the arrival of the private medical jet. After several awkward and tactful explanations of why Robert would not be staying at this so-called hospital, he was successfully delivered to our van and headed for the nearest airport. It must have looked like a reenactment of the Battle of Normandy the way he hobbled out, wincing in pain as his arms draped across mine and Victoria's shoulders.

The drive from the so-called hospital to the airport was performed in the same post-armed-bank-robbery disregard for acceptable traffic patterns and laws as before. Our mission was again singular: get Robert to the tarmac. By this point, I misremember myself having a bandana around my forehead and a cigarette hanging from my lip as our tires screeched towards the runway. Just like a Jason Bourne movie, the plane touched down the very instant our van crashed through the locked gates of the airport. Sparks flew, and police lights raced behind us, but we weren't going to stop before we made it to the awaiting jet. The true version of my memory had less dramatic appeal, but the adrenaline I felt pointed towards something more exciting and dangerous.

Once Robert was safely boarded onto the jet, we could rest knowing the doctors on board were medically trained and able to take care of him long enough to get him back to an American hospital. After many hours of flying and a proper medical diagnosis, doctors told Robert he had a gallbladder rupture, and a simple surgery to remove the organ would solve his problems. After just a week, he was back in Ukraine and acting as if nothing had happened.

Robert's journey taught me a valuable lesson. Despite my doubt and reservations, God provided for Robert's needs. I understand there were a few things in Robert's favor. It is clear his financial standing allowed him to get a private medical jet to take him back to better medical care in America, but I also know God provided those means for him.

If you're like me, you can't afford a private jet to take you anywhere for any reason. However, that fact shouldn't shield you or me from knowing the Lord takes care of His people. There have been countless times in my life when something works out in my favor for no other plausible reason than God designed it that way. I would imagine if you took the time to examine your life, you'd see the same providence in your experiences.

The thing is, God's Word talks about how He's for His people. His love, care, attention, and desires are for His creation, and we're part of that. This isn't to say every situation will turn out in exactly our favor or the way we wished it would. The Lord looks at you and me with glowing eyes and compassion, which exceeds my understanding. Neither I, nor you, deserve the grace and mercy the Lord extends to us daily, but the Lord remains faithful to us.

There is no amount of earthly pain or suffering that can reduce God's affection for us. He knows our limits and, I believe, allows us to go right to the edge of them at times. We all face struggles and circumstances that are painful, but the Lord has promised to not let go of us. If we believe that, we view life's challenges in a different light. Instead of the problem at hand being about us, we can shift the focus to Jesus and understand He orchestrates events for His glory.

Just like in Robert's crisis, I see God working in my life in ways that I don't understand. It seems more and more often that I sense God asking me to trust Him with my circumstances no matter how outlandish or helpless they may seem. When I think of God, I often picture His arms stretched towards me. All I can hear Him say is, "I know you're hurting, but just trust Me."

If you're like me, you sometimes fall prey to the lies that you can do life on your own, or even worse, that Jesus isn't enough. I don't have all the answers, but I know enough to understand that without trusting in the Lord's help and providence, I can surrender all of my hopes, dreams, and desires and abandon any semblance of rescue or salvation.

When times get tough, and things begin to seem impossible, remember the Lord is for His people. In your darkest hour, in the times when you look to the horizon and don't see hope, know God is sitting there beside you, waiting on you to look His way. Whether you sense it or not, His arm is draped across your shoulders as He whispers, "Let's do this together." Whether it's a medical jet that lands in a foreign country or simply a hug from a friend, the Lord provides hope and love, which far surpasses our understanding and timing.

Believe God when He says He hears your cries for help. He loves you, and He looks towards you with patience, understanding, and grace. Trust Him.

Mafia Men

**I used to think Jesus looks at me in
disappointment. I now know He looks at me as
His beloved and a source of His joy.**

Each fall, the village I lived in held a huge event celebrating another year of its existence. The village's "club" was transformed into a meeting space fit for all village residents. From what I could tell, it didn't matter what anyone did or didn't have planned for the day; if you lived in the village, your attendance was expected. After all, everyone who lived in the village was known by name and couldn't fly under the radar if they tried.

The event planners were the elderly women in the village. They dressed up in fancy dresses, did their hair up, and arrived at the village club looking ready to party. As Ukrainian culture allows, or even promulgates, the women and all of the party's attendees arrived with ample amounts of alcohol and tobacco. There must have been a private pre-game celebration nearby at one of the village homes. As people began to pour in, it was clear they had already begun the assault on their livers for the celebration ahead.

The village club wasn't anything special. There were no modern attractions within, and there wasn't even glass in the windows or doors in the doorways. For some reason, power had been wired throughout the club at some point in its existence, but I wouldn't volunteer to be the one to plug anything in. Electric shock was part of the equation for whoever accepted the challenge of connecting a power cord to the outlet.

When I arrived at the village club, the elderly ladies had already shown the DJ where to set up. As I walked in, he was standing in the corner with a card table supporting his 1980s-era cassette player. Behind him was a tall stack of cassette tapes and a bottle of beer. It didn't seem to matter that not many people had arrived for the party; this man was dedicated to his craft and was in full party mode.

Unfamiliar techno beats rattled through the sub-par speakers into an almost empty room. The DJ did not have a professional rig, nor did he have speakers much louder than the phone in your pocket. I'm sure he understood these truths, but it didn't seem to bother him. He was simply there to provide the best experience with what he had. I admired that about him.

The elderly village ladies were busy gossiping and arguing about where to put the refreshments. Like the DJ, they too had only small card tables set around the room intended for drinks and finger-foods to be placed upon them. As other village members began to arrive, I noticed it wasn't clear party-goers were expected to bring a small dish to add to the mix. Villagers would enter the club, notice the growing tables of food and quietly dip out headed towards the nearby village store to retrieve a whole dried fish or bag of chips. This happened without fail to each newcomer, and it was rather comical to observe.

Similar to most gatherings I have been to in America, the women congregated in one area, and men separated themselves into another. It was clear everyone knew each other, but some people were more acquainted with each other than the rest. Hugs and handshakes were shared, as were smiles and laughs.

Most everyone in the crowd had a bottle of beer or vodka in their hands, and nobody seemed to be out of place. As a casual observer, it seemed everyone was the best of friends and enjoyed each other's company.

Before long, Adam and Charlotte arrived, and they too hurried off to the village store before making their official entrance to the party. The small village shop did not have too much variety, so we were undoubtedly in the repeat refreshment category now. After returning, Adam and Charlotte hugged necks and shook hands, and resigned themselves to the opposite corner of the DJ. The celebration was intended for lifelong village residents, and it was difficult not to feel like an outsider on a day like this.

After several hours of celebration, I began to wonder how long the event would last. It was clear most of the village residents had no intention of slowing their alcohol intake or self-expression of dance. For Adam, Charlotte, and myself–the only three not participating in these things–the celebration seemed to drone on. I didn't want to be rude and certainly didn't want to mark myself as ungrateful after being invited to the village gathering, so I resolved my intentions to stay as long as the party carried on.

Several hours after the party had begun, a black BMW sedan pulled up in front of the village club. On a few occasions, similar looking cars had visited Adam's house. Each time a fancy car visited our home, a few burly men knocked on our door and made vague threats about our Christian camp in exchange for a few bucks. It didn't happen often, but when the so-called "mafia men" visited, it was cause for the hair to stand up on my arms. Interactions with those mafia men made me feel dirty and fearful for what would happen if we didn't comply with their extortions. I didn't like when they visited and I didn't want them at our village party.

After a quick read of the room, it was clear to me I wasn't alone in my reservations about the car that had just pulled up. The music seemed to stop abruptly, as did the dancing. Men carefully and quietly walked to the windows as they gently set their glass beer bottles down. They intently looked towards the BMW, now idling out in front of our celebration.

For several minutes, the car and the men in the village club held their positions. Nobody moved, and everybody's tension levels rose. As my fears of a visit from the mafia men grew, I became frozen with fear and anticipation. I glanced to my right and left to the men standing at the windows in search of comfort or relief. They offered nothing of the sort. Instead, they deflected my glances with a continual fixation on the black BMW still stationary in front of the village club.

Then, slowly, the driver door of the parked black BMW opened. The person opening the door wasn't sure of their decision to expose themselves to the elements outside of the car, but they had begun the process nonetheless. After the door was fully open, nobody appeared in the threshold. Instead, the passenger door followed the same hesitant pattern as the driver's door and reluctantly opened. Next, the two rear passenger doors opened in the same fashion. All four car doors were now open, but none of the vehicle's occupants had presented themselves outside of the car.

I began replaying all of the Jason Bourne and James Bond films I had ever seen and wished I had paid more attention in karate class as a kid. I imagined what was next to come was rapid gunfire and sure death. It was clear to me nobody around me had any idea why the black BMW was parked in front of our village celebration. The car certainly did not belong in our village, but it didn't seem to have any intention of leaving either.

After what felt like hours of fearful anticipation, a dark-headed man with a thick gut appeared in the doorway of the driver's door. He simply looked towards the direction of the village clubhouse. His eyes periodically stopped as they surveyed the crowd. He didn't say anything, and he didn't make any gestures.

Several quiet minutes passed as each of the remaining men inside the car slowly and cautiously presented themselves outside the vehicle just as the driver had done. With each new figure emerging, there seemed to be no new information. Each man simply stood up straight and faced our village club. As each minute passed, my fear of extortion shrunk as the anticipation of my kidnapping grew.

Thoughts raced through my mind. I wondered if they were with the mafia and looking for me, Adam, or Charlotte. I was sure I'd spend the rest of my days in a gulag, or even worse, a grave in Ukraine. Time didn't allow for a comprehensive evaluation of what was going on, but fear certainly made a home in my brain.

Quick flicks of my eyes left and right towards other villagers did not provide any relief. In most cases, my eyes were met with the same fear and uncertainty that my gaze was surely portraying. Still, there were no words exchanged between anyone present at the gathering, and the music and been shut off completely. There was total silence.

I wanted to run, but I had nowhere to go. It seemed like a sure death sentence to run within sight of the four strange men in front of me. My sentiment must have been shared with other local village men as a break in silence erupted. Without planning or preparation, it seemed a group of village men at once decided to approach the mafia men now standing before the village club. Thankfully, the village men approached them with outstretched hands and warm spirits instead of hostility and violence. Had it been the latter, I'm not sure how much help I would have been.

The mafia men responded by exchanging heated words with the villagers, and it was clear they weren't there to attend the celebration. I didn't understand all that was said and likely couldn't repeat it if I had, but it was clear calming our village's visitors would be an uphill battle. My fears began to subside as I heard the distinctive intoxicated slur in the visitors' speech as they continued interacting with the village residents now standing before them. The four men didn't seem to be concerned with finding anyone in particular, and it now seemed more plausible they just wanted to make trouble.

As the village men approached the four strangers standing outside of their BMW, all four strange men jumped back into their vehicle in a haste. The driver cranked the car and threw the transmission into drive. As dust and pebbles violently flew out behind the vehicle, the car traveled a few hundred feet and abruptly stopped again. This time, the car was sideways and blocking the only entrance and exit to our village. All four doors flew open again, and each man quickly exited and crossed their arms as they stood amid the settling dust and chaos around them.

The peaceful village men began to cautiously approach the four strangers again. This time, the recent occupants of the BMW shouted and demanded the villagers stayed back. I was still at a loss for which words were being spoken, but I could tell the four strange men were growing more hostile with the village people.

An evening bus now headed towards our village bus stop. It was clear the black BMW would not be allowing the bus to continue past, and the bus driver began to honk its horn. The men standing outside of the BMW divided their attention between the bus and the village members, but they treated both parties with the same amount of disrespect and hostility. As far as I could tell, the BMW's former occupants were not making any threats or demands. They seemed content with merely causing a scene and making everyone's lives around them more difficult.

I don't advocate for drunk driving, but I was happy to realize these men had drunkenly ventured out from their homes in the city and into the downtrodden streets of the village I lived in. By this stage of our interaction, it was clear that our visitors were nothing more than a bunch of intoxicated idiots based on their unsteady steps and incoherent words. It was increasingly evident the threat I had once assumed imminent was really just a bunch of lost and inarticulate guys.

As the four drunk provocateurs and the city bus continued in their stand-off, the village men again began to approach the car's former occupants. There was a lot of shouting and finger-pointing coming from the BMW's former occupants, but ultimately, it seemed the village men simply wanted to talk with the angry men. From my vantage point, the village men's open arms and inviting gestures were met with hostile retreats and clenched fists from the guys standing beside the BMW.

The village men were inviting the angry men to join us in our village celebration and attempting to disarm them with overt and obvious gestures of hospitality. The village men didn't recognize the strangers who arrived in the BMW, but they seemed to want to get to know our visitors and welcome them into our gathering. From the village men's perspective, we had plenty of food and drink to share with the strangers, so it seemed appropriate to invite them to our party. Based on the strange men's body language and quick decision to jump back in their vehicle, they didn't seem ready to join us at our gathering.

After the BMW vanished over the horizon of our village, I sunk into my chair with relief. I realized the threat to my personal safety had passed, but I was left with a lesson. What I had experienced that day wasn't an overt threat to my life, but the four strange men had threatened my idea of community and celebration. Those strange men arrived at our doorstep with the simple goal of creating chaos and concern among the people celebrating within the village. I can't be sure, but it seems as if the men knew our village was hosting a special celebration and they felt threatened by it. I have no idea where these men lived or exactly where they came from, but I know they wanted to disrupt our day and our plans.

Looking back, I think many people in our lives resemble the four strange men in the black BMW. If we're honest with ourselves, we likely have been one of the four men ourselves. If you're like me, you can think back to times in your life when there was someone, or a group of people, participating in a celebration or set of events that you weren't invited to. In some cases, the celebration at hand was something you desperately wanted to be a part of. In other cases, you've probably stumbled into a gathering and were reminded of your loneliness. Human nature is filled with the desire to be around other people and to feel accepted, and it hurts when we're rejected or not even invited.

As you go through life, you will undoubtedly encounter instances of rejection and disapproval. In some cases, these things can be of value as long as they are coming from people you trust and who love you. We all need course correction from time to time, and often the best people for that are those who are closest to you. Other times, rejection and disapproval remind us we live in a fallen world, and there are a lot of imperfect people around us.

Unlike the four strange men in the black BMW, I hope you go through life looking for ways to celebrate those around you even when you weren't invited to the party. This won't always be easy, but the results speak loudly. To celebrate those around you, especially in circumstances where you weren't thought of or invited, displays a love that is exponentially higher than your own preservation or glorification. When you celebrate the achievements, plans, goals, or victories of the people around you, it requires you to think less of yourself and more of them.

It can be difficult, but I encourage you to look for ways to lift those around you higher than yourself. Just like the four strange men in the black BMW, you will drive past parties you weren't invited to. You'll also learn of people who are more successful or better situated in life than you are. If you look to those people– the ones who churn emotions of disgust, envy, and anger–and decide to welcome and celebrate them, you'll not only find greater joy in your own life, but you'll also leave those around you with a reminder of who Christ is.

There will undoubtedly be people in your life, like the mafia men, who are difficult to deal with. You'll probably even want to tell a few of them to get lost. But, Jesus lived His life on earth with open arms just like the villagers extended theirs towards the mafia men. That same Jesus is alive today and has an open-door policy. Just as the village men invited the strangers into our party, Jesus looks at you and me and invites us to His eternal celebration with an outstretched hand. You can't grab someone's hand with a clinched fist, so show your palms to the people around you instead.

Dim Fireworks
I now look at my reflection and remember God knows what's buried deepest and still loves me.

I 've lived a large part of my life in Alabama, where the weather is generally hot and humid with not a lot of snow. Every few years, the state gets lucky enough to see a flurry or two fall, but it's hardly ever enough to build a snowman or have a snowball fight. Instead, if *any* amount of snow falls in Alabama, the entire state acts like it's doomsday, and we all stay home from work and school. Everyone rushes to buy milk and bread as if those items offer superior nourishment. I've never understood the bread and milk move; I've always opted for frozen pizzas and ice cream for the possibility of my last meal.

One year it *actually* snowed in Alabama, and thousands of people got stranded at work. The local officials warned the roads had become "impassable," so naturally, a bunch of people hopped into their cars to find out for themselves. I knew many of these brave souls. In fact, they were the ones who told me what it feels like to live in a car on the side of the roadway for three days straight because the roads truly had become impassable. Luckily, I heeded the advice of the meteorologist and stayed home.

Ukraine's weather is much different than Alabama's. It

snows a lot there. If you don't adequately prepare for the heavy snow before it comes, you'll likely find yourself unable to get out of your house for real. Most people I knew in Ukraine hated the snow. They'd been around it their entire lives and didn't see any fun or whimsy when the snow began to fall each year. To them, it was just another obstacle to overcome in their daily lives. Not for me, though. I *loved* the snow and eagerly awaited its arrival.

As a kid from Alabama, I'd dreamed of having a White Christmas, but I was let down year after year. There were a few years here and there when it was *slightly* possible to see a few flurries on Christmas day, but I think it happened only once in my life. Unlike in America, Christmas isn't widely celebrated in Ukraine. Ukraine as a whole isn't too big on the whole Jesus thing, although some families still celebrate more from a cultural perspective. New Years is the *big* holiday in Ukraine. Everyone goes all out. People have parties filled with cakes, friends, families, and often, more booze than is advisable. I guess it's not too different than how Americans celebrate New Year's, but it felt like Ukrainians bypassed Christmas to save their energy and excitement for the first day of the year.

By the time New Year's came around in Ukraine, there had been snow on the ground for months. There were rarely days warm enough to melt the snow, so it got deeper and deeper with each snowstorm that rolled through. The city's main roads frequently had trucks drive through with large snowplows mounted to the front, which piled the snow high on the edges of the roadway. In the village, the snow plowing was left to locals with tractors. These trucks and tractors made snow piles that were taller than I am. If you fell in, it might be spring until you're found.

I liked the snow. To me, there was a certain magic in the air when the snow fell. Everything seemed quieter, and my thoughts clearer. I enjoyed bundling up and walking throughout the city as it snowed. Although whenever the snow fell, I often did too. My eyes weren't too good at telling the difference between ice and snow, but my butt often let me know the difference.

Adam and his family went back to the States for Christmas and New Year's, and Steven did the same. Not much happens in the village of Novopavlivka any time of the year, but especially not during the winter. Our camp wasn't equipped to house kids in the harsh winter conditions, so we had to wait until early spring to host them again. Most people who live in the village resign themselves to staying close to their fireplace and not leaving their homes unless absolutely necessary. I figured I didn't have much business staying in the village while Adam wasn't there.

Instead, I asked Steven if I could stay in his apartment in the city while he, too, was back in America. Thankfully, Steven agreed and tossed me the keys to his place and told me he'd be back sometime in February. That's how Steven operated. He communicated in loose and uncertain terms, but I didn't mind his vague timeline. I'd at least have access to grocery stores and the occasional conversation with a human while staying at Steven's place.

Soon after moving into Steven's apartment in late December, I came to the painful realization that his apartment did not have heat. His apartment was so small that a hairdryer would have done the trick, but it didn't have one of those either. The apartment was built when Ukraine was part of the Soviet Union. If you don't know much about that time in Ukraine's part of the world, almost everything was bare and drab.

Steven's apartment had a few metal pipes that lined the walls, which sometimes had hot water slowly circulating through them. The idea was the little amount of heat radiating from the metal pipes would be enough to warm a room. As you can imagine, these pipes were about as useful as lighting a candle in a room in hopes of providing warmth and comfort. I spent most of my time layered in winter clothing and slept in a sleeping bag zipped up far enough for only my head to be exposed. Being inside wasn't much different than being outside. Still, I was grateful to be in the city instead of the village for a while, so I had little to complain about.

During my stay in Steven's apartment, one of my daily activities was walking to the grocery store. I used this daily trip to get groceries for my meals, but more importantly, to provide something to look forward to in my routine. In addition to the brutal winter temperatures and heavy snowfall, the sun set a little after three o'clock during this part of winter. Seasonal depression was a reality in these conditions, and I desperately needed something to draw my attention towards something productive. Since walking to the store required careful planning and even more careful foot placement, it was always a task that took longer than it should.

Each day, I'd gear up and mentally prepare myself for what was to come. I was sure to encounter a few dicey characters on my journey due to the nearby drug rehabilitation facility, and I knew I'd spend a considerable amount of time on my backside due to the slick roads. From the days of hanging out with Steven at his place in the summer, I knew the street he lived on had a few uncapped needles lying around. I guess the people going to and from the drug rehab place didn't need them anymore and had no problem leaving them in the street. I was always nervous with the deep snow that I'd one day find one of these needles during one of my involuntary trips to the ground, but thankfully, that never happened.

After a few trips to the store, I wised up and began wearing an extra layer of pants with some socks in the back pockets to lessen the blow each time my butt met the earth. I looked like

Ralphie from *A Christmas Story*, and truthfully, I let one of his brother's infamous words slip once or twice as I hit the ground. The falls continued to be painful and took me off guard each time, but at least my back end wasn't bruising anymore. Thankfully, I was in a foreign country, and nobody understood me when my colorful language livened up my drab surroundings.

On New Year's Eve, I found myself walking to the grocery store. Being the start of a new year, I wanted to cook myself a special meal, one that would take a while to prepare. I figured if I spent all afternoon going to the store, cooking, and then finally eating, my mind would be occupied by chores instead of missing out on the celebrations which filled the streets below. With a plan in mind, I suited up, mentally prepared myself for the inevitable falls, and started my trek.

Predictably, my journey to the grocery store was met with involuntary breaks spent sitting on the ground with a few laughs and fingers aimed in my direction from the locals. By the Lord's grace, I eventually made it back from the grocery store with a bag full of food fit for a celebration of one. By this point of my journey in Ukraine, I had learned a few more Russian words than I had known when I first bought milk, but I always seemed to learn new Russian vocabulary in the aisles of the grocery store. Trips to the store were now a bit more manageable, but I still avoided the cashier who first helped me.

Steven's kitchen was the smallest room in his apartment, but one I felt most comforted in. I could stretch each of my four limbs out and touch all four walls of his kitchen simultaneously. The kitchen had a gas stovetop, a sink, a mini-fridge, and a small cabinet big enough to fit a jar of peanut butter and a cereal box. In desperate times when the weather was exceedingly cold, I would light the gas burner on the stove and huddle around it for warmth. This practice was incredibly dangerous, but I was sure to freeze to death without it, so it seemed like a well-calculated risk.

After getting back from the store, I found myself in Steven's kitchen, feeling a bit lonely. As I stood in the kitchen with a bag of groceries, the fact I was cooking only for myself on this day of celebration began to sink in. I had observed people in the store together, and it reminded me of my isolation. What I really wanted was to share my meal with a friend, but I understood the chances of that were nonexistent.

After cooking my elaborate dinner of cheap steak, potatoes, and vegetables, I found myself sitting in the kitchen, looking out of the window towards the growing crowds below. With the kitchen light on, I could only see my reflection unless I cupped my hands around my face as I peered out. Regardless, the celebrations on the street drew my attention out of the window. I sat there with a half-satisfied stomach, a flood of emotions, and longing questions. I wondered, "What in the world am I doing in Ukraine?" I questioned if I had made a mistake.

As I was sitting in my self-doubt and depression, the clock ticked towards midnight, and fireworks began exploding in the night sky. I could hear people spilling into the streets, laughing and enjoying the company of others. I wished so desperately to be back in America surrounded by my friends and family, just like the people in the streets below.

During my time in Ukraine, there were a handful of instances when I questioned what I was doing so far from home. If I allowed myself to dwell on it, I found myself sinking into thoughts of how foolish and ill-advised my decision was to move 5500 miles from home at seventeen years old. Of the times I can remember, sitting in Steven's kitchen on New Year's Eve was my worst battle with those thoughts. My doubts were painful and discouraging.

As I sat feeling depressed, I pulled out my phone to text a

Ukrainian friend who lived in a city a few hours away. My Russian writing skills were limited and elementary, and I didn't have the crutch of reading body language to help me navigate my conversation. My friend and I communicated in simple terms for a few minutes, but eventually, my lack of ability to express myself in Russian deepened my negative feelings, and I stopped replying. I was trying desperately to climb out of the emotional hole I was in, but it felt like my clawing only crumbled the walls around me, burying me deeper.

After several minutes of sitting in silence, I decided to find a way to accept my situation. No matter how much I wanted things to be different that night, my situation wasn't going to change. I realized I wasn't going to magically appear at a party, and my friends and family weren't going to knock on Steven's apartment door. As I sat in Steven's kitchen, I began to pray God would show me a deeper meaning in the situation I was in. I didn't expect His message to be spelled out in the fireworks, which continued to explode around me, but I simply wanted to feel connected and remembered.

If you're like me, you can sometimes feel distant from God and even from those physically near you. Many of us experience these types of feelings and resolve it's a "me" problem. I can't possibly know your situation better than you, but I would argue God sometimes allows us to feel separated or distant from Him long enough to demonstrate His love for us. On the face of it, that sounds a little backwards. It doesn't make much sense for God to push us away or allow us to drift from Him, but I think there's a God-glorying aspect to it.

In the times I remember feeling distant from God, just as I did on New Year's Eve in Ukraine, I often find myself running back towards God in desperation. In my experience, there's an undeniable comfort in being close to God. Still, for some reason, I repeatedly find myself drifting from Him. I've always attributed this pattern to my naturally introverted tendencies. I often want my personal space, but I've come to realize closeness to God is important as well.

As I get older, I look back to feelings of isolation and realize I was chasing a particular financial goal, work promotion, or simply my own selfish desires, and it often led me to feel less whole. At times, the pursuit of what I want is void of Christ's direction, and I find myself longing for a deeper connection with Him as a result. Jesus knows this about me and sits patiently with His arms open, ready to embrace me. Sometimes it just takes a while for my stubborn nature to break down enough for me to see Him sitting there waiting.

Deep down, I know God was sitting right beside me in Steven's apartment on New Year's Eve in Ukraine. I didn't realize it at the time, but Christ was enough to sustain me even as I stared out of the window towards crowds of jubilant people ringing in the New Year. God delights in our fellowship with others, but He is also overjoyed when we seek Him above everything else. Just like I was trying to do by going to the grocery store and cooking a big meal, we often do things in our life with the sole purpose of distracting ourselves. Sometimes we realize we're doing it, and other times we remain willfully blind.

We're often afraid to be still long enough to feel Jesus in the room with us, so we intentionally lock the door to keep Him out. We know our pasts, our sins, and our shortcomings. We trick ourselves into thinking God doesn't know these things about us too. Falling short of God's glory makes us feel dirty and shameful, especially when we hide from the redeeming love Christ offers despite our mistakes. The real self-evaluation and course correction happens in the presence of God. Only then can we see the perfect example Jesus set for us and begin to tune our image to better reflect His.

Just like New Year's night in Ukraine, I sometimes find

myself hiding from God. I don't want to acknowledge how He sees the good, the bad, and the ugly in me. I too often choose to fabricate things to distract me from being one-on-one with Him. We don't leave room in our schedules to be quiet, still, or reflective. Instead, we focus on our calendars, our goals, or simply our couches. Just like I did as I cupped my hands around my face looking out of the window in Steven's kitchen, we too often go out of our way to see outside the windows of our lives instead of quietly sitting back and examining our own reflections. We would rather look past our own lives and long for what others are participating in around us.

I don't think God faults us for trying to avoid what's most important in our lives. It seems more plausible that He knows the pain and discomfort, which is often associated with looking at ourselves in the window's reflection. This truth is one of the main reasons for the Cross too. Jesus knows we need a way for hope to appear in our reflection, and that is something we can never do on our own. We need someone to look to, someone who can offer us a helping hand.

If you're like me, pride plays a massive role in denying we need help from time to time. None of us are built to go through life alone without God's help. I'm still a work in progress, just like you are. But, instead of looking past myself in the reflection of a window to watch dim fireworks explode, I now see myself and remember God knows what's buried deepest within me and still loves me. With that in mind, I can now look at myself in a window's reflection and smile, knowing I'm His and He's mine.

Hardly a Harley
We can all learn to take the slower route towards our destination if it means reaching out and grabbing a few hands along the way.

oing places within Ukraine is a long process if you don't have private transportation. City buses, long train rides, and even short hops on small planes are commonplace. I have to imagine this isn't unique to Ukraine, but living abroad introduced me to the route planning and time budgeting necessary to get to where I was going in a timely manner.

Throughout my stay in Ukraine, I spent countless hours standing at bus stops around the city and in various villages. I was often accompanied by a Ukrainian local, normally middle-aged and always smoking a cigarette and drinking a beer while crouching just above the earth's surface. Bus stops in Ukraine were a social thing. After all, it's what connected everyone as they went throughout their daily routines.

The bus stop in my village was an old one. The street leading to it was an abused dirt road that had not been properly maintained throughout its existence. Trash and other littered objects were fixtures around this bus stop. There was an old bench under a makeshift awning, but sitting down meant risking getting splinters in places you'd rather not have them. Waiting at the bus stop felt uncomfortable and uneasy.

I often felt guilty when I was standing at this bus stop because I was often accompanied by an elderly lady who was in no shape to stand and wait outside. I don't know where this lady went every day or if she had anybody who could go for her. I wondered if she felt the same way I did about the bus stop. I'm sure she understood the graffiti scribbled across the bus stop better than I could, and I sometimes wondered if what it said bothered her. If the constant cigarette smoke and broken beer bottles didn't faze her, maybe she could look past the curse words written above her head.

There were a few bus routes which came through my village. Many of them connected from other villages because we were fortunate enough to have a small village store where you could buy a few grocery necessities. Many people from surrounding villages came daily to buy bread, butter, or beer. Due to our little store acting as a travel hub, we had many people in and out of our village each day. Many of the people the bus delivered were your everyday type of person. They simply had a few things on their to-do list, and my village was a checkmark on their list.

Other passengers were on more of the seedy side, probably the same people who broke beer bottles and wrote curse words on our dilapidated bus stop. Many of these people arrived in my village as a daily ritual. The clerk at the village store knew each of the men by name and seemed not bothered by their daily company.

During the warmer months, men sat out front with a plastic cup full of tan beer, and none of them wore a shirt. Their bellies were bloated, and their skin burned by the summer sun. The men were always loud and didn't seem to care much if anyone observed them, not even me as a foreigner. My Russian language skills were in constant growth while I lived in Ukraine, but I never rose to the level of understanding a drunk Ukrainian man.

The bus system in Ukraine was a utility for me. I depended on it to get me to where I was going if I wasn't traveling with Adam. In the beginning, I memorized only the bus numbers, not the street or village names displayed on the white office paper taped to the side of the bus. Learning which bus delivered me to various locations became a math equation. If I took the "4" bus from my village but wanted to go on the "13" bus to the city, I needed to get a total of "17" points to get me there. With my faulty logic, I sometimes got a different combination of numbers which happened to equal "17" and ended up in a place where I didn't know anyone, nor how to get back to where I belonged.

After a few trial and error runs, I developed another indicator of whether I had been successful in choosing the correct bus. I learned that buses passing through busy hubs would be the most congested. As the buses became more and more crowded along a route, there came the point when all of the seats were taken. When the buses got full enough to be standing room only, the passengers in the center of the bus were forced to either hold onto the overhead railing or fall backwards into their fellow passengers' laps. I realized if I was headed for the city and never had to stand up, I was likely going in the wrong direction.

This sort of compromise wasn't a big deal for passengers aboard a bus when it was cold outside. However, the sun beat down relentlessly upon fellow travelers in the warmer months as they stood patiently waiting on a bus, and this meant unmitigated nasal assault once those travelers were aboard. Just like most local cars, the buses did not have the luxury of having an A/C unit. This fact, coupled with the unfortunate truth that many Ukrainian men wore cut off shirts and didn't care much for deodorant, meant the buses often became traveling bombs of intense body odor. No matter how many windows were cracked, the stench of a bus full of sweaty people left a sting in my nostril and a pit in my stomach.

One day, during my wait for a bus in the city, pigeons above me decided to use my sleeve as their toilet. Unfortunately, I was wearing a white shirt when my misfortune occurred, and the locals around me were jubilant amidst my humiliation. I couldn't understand all of the words being hurled at me, but I could gather based on the extended pointer fingers and laughter that the jokes were at my expense. As my shoulder became a public reminder that I was waiting on a bus, I began to wonder if there was a better option to get me to where I needed to go.

After living in Ukraine for a while and experiencing a few more public displays of the pitfalls of waiting at bus stops, I found myself wanting my own form of transportation. Predictably, I grew tired of stuffing my nose with cotton balls just to get from one destination to the next, and I wanted the freedom to move about on more of a whim. I knew I didn't have enough money for an actual car, nor could I get a license, so I began to toss around the idea of a motorcycle.

Under Ukrainian law, I didn't need a driver's license to operate a motorcycle, so I figured it was my only option. I had grown up riding dirt bikes, and I felt fairly comfortable on two wheels. Granted, almost all of my time spent on two motorized wheels was spent off-road without the concern of other cars or traffic laws. Still, I was confident I could navigate Ukrainian roads with my arms outstretched to handlebars and a motor humming beneath me.

I had grand visions of owning a loud, rumbling motorcycle with a fat rear tire that screamed "awesome." Even before moving to Ukraine, I had dreamed of owning a bike that would take me 0-60mph in just a few short seconds, or one that would force me to only its rear wheel if I was too aggressive with the throttle. I didn't realize it at the time, but those bikes were way out of my price range. I was in more of the "glorified moped" price point. My dad and I had agreed beforehand on a price we–I mean he–was willing to pay for a private mode of transportation without cutting into the money I had raised for my adventure in Ukraine. I was thankful for his generosity, but like any teenage boy, I was hoping he would have agreed to spend just a few thousand more. My price range would afford me an annoying high pitch screech and a back tire about as wide as a high school textbook. What I would be buying was hardly a Harley.

After taking the bus to the nearest local motorcycle dealership, I squared my expectations with the $500 I was willing to spend on a private mode of transportation. I was humbled. After a few poorly worded and head-scratching attempts at haggling with the Ukrainian salesman, I found myself shaking hands in front of a sad excuse of a motorcycle. The deal was done; I had bought a two-wheeled motorized mode of transportation. Even though I was buying less than what I had hoped for, I was proud to hand over the equivalent of $500 in cash to the salesman and be handed the keys to my new ride.

With my newfound keys in hand and a helmet fit for a kid on training wheels, I cranked my bike for the first time. After a few sputters and clanks, the bike sprang into action with a puff of black smoke shooting from the tailpipe. As I sat on the bike, trying to look cool, I gave the throttle a few short revs as the bike made an intensifying buzzing sound. The bike sounded more like an angry hornet than it did a motorcycle. I'm sure the salesman looked at me with amusement as I imagined myself as Evil Knievel about to jump across the Grand Canyon. I was happy and full of testosterone as I revved my new bike.

My journey back to my village took several hours and was

filled with tightly gripped steering and urgent pleas for safety as I navigated the seemingly incomprehensible flow of traffic. My dinky helmet provided no relief for the dust thrown in my face by the passing cars and busses as I puttered back to my side of town. I would have welcomed the high lifted putrid arms I was accustomed to on the city buses over the sheer terror I experienced while traveling Ukraine's open roads.

As I pulled back into my village, I tried to act calm and collected. I gave a few proud and confident waves to the people I passed at the bus stop and puttered on towards Adam's house. Adam must have anticipated the quality of my journey because he was standing in front of the house with a grin on his face as I arrived. I pulled my new bike into the driveway and flicked the kickstand down as I removed the dust-soaked helmet from my head. His only question was, "How'd it go?"

Perceiving an invitation to dig deeper into my journey, I quickly replied with a simple, "Fine," as I got busy dusting off my new ride. Adam and I both knew the trip was less than fine, but he was gracious enough not to press it further and allowed me to rest for a few minutes in peace.

Over the next several months, I spent many hours guiding my motorcycle towards various missions and adventures. I traveled to nearby villages, to the city, and to simply get lost with purposeful intent from time to time. My motorcycle became a source of comfort and refuge when my inner introvert rose to the surface. I was thankful to have the means to escape for a short time and take in what was around me as I puttered down local roads. When I rode my motorcycle, I allowed my mind to consider what Ukraine was teaching me. The daily distractions and setbacks seemed to disappear for a short while as I scurried down old dirt roads and uncharted paths. Life was simple and good when I was riding my motorcycle.

Ukrainian traffic patterns are a little less structured than what I was accustomed to in America. In my home country, speed limits and direction of travel are clearly defined, and often times, heavily enforced. To my surprise, Ukraine didn't have such rigid traffic guidelines, at least not ones that were enforced with the threat of citations or jail time. When I got pulled over in Ukraine, the policeman would insinuate he could look past whatever grave infraction I had committed if I'd simply slide a few bucks his way in a handshake. This happened to me on multiple occasions, and each one seemed to be equally status quo and corrupt. Being a foreigner, I didn't want to challenge the system, so I felt little choice other than to fall in line.

Once I got outside of the village roads, the main road to the city developed into a four-lane highway, which was split by a grass median. The speed limit on this road was technically low enough for cars and buses to travel along it safely; however, I never once saw a policeman on the road enforcing anything traffic-related if it didn't fit his ploy for a bribe. This road was known to locals as a dangerous highway, but it was the only main road connecting villages to the city. Most people traveled this road on a weekly basis as carefully as possible, but some drivers treated the road as the Autobahn. It was best to say a prayer before setting off towards my destination if this particular road was in my path.

During one of my journeys, I came across a horrific accident. It's one of those scenes that you never really erase from your memory. It becomes a permanent scar on your conscience, one that visits you while you're sleeping and makes you watch again before being allowed to wake up. The incident happened one afternoon while I was headed into town. As I was traveling towards the city, traffic stopped abruptly in front of me. Looking ahead through the few cars that provided a barrier between me and the chaos, it was clear something significant had occurred, and people were in a panic. As I edged closer to the front of the traffic line, my eyes connected with the source of terror and shock.

In front of me laid two people who were clearly dead. Their motorcycle was a few hundred yards away, and a sedan with a severely dented hood idled just beyond the deceased. The driver of the involved sedan was in sheer panic and disbelief as he paced around, grabbing brief glances of the scene while trying to calm his nerves and conscience. It was apparent the collision was a mistake based on the busted tire of the sedan. The man who hit the two individuals on the motorcycle head-on didn't mean to cause the pain and harm he had, but there was nothing he could do, or any of us could do, at that point. Even though the motorcycle riders lost their lives, I have to imagine the driver of the sedan lost something about himself that day too.

As I watched in unspeakable terror, my body began to shake. I prayed for the two people now lying motionless on the ground as their blood spilled around them and their shapes remained unrecognizable. I reasoned with God as to why this had to happen and pleaded for His hand to intervene, but I knew their fate had been sealed. I felt sad for the man in the sedan. I could only imagine what I felt as a passerby must have been multiplied within him. I wanted to hug him and let him know he would be alright, but I couldn't bring my body to move towards him.

It was evident in this instance the man's car was of no value to him. He didn't care about the damage to his hood and would likely trade anything for the outcome to be different. In that moment, not only was his perception of life and the finality of earthly death on display, but mine was as well. He and I shared the same desire for a different outcome, but we both knew there was nothing we could do to change the situation.

Although I wish it happened under different circumstances,

God taught me a valuable lesson that day. For months, I wanted a quicker, more private, and more convenient way of travel. I didn't want to have to stand and wait at a bus stop or put up with pungent body odor as I traveled on a city bus. I wanted time for myself and to be distant from others. My motorcycle provided a stiff arm towards the people around me, and I grew to despise that fact. The accident I witnessed undoubtedly impacted my decision to get rid of my bike, but choosing to embrace the people around me caused me to toss the keys to someone else for good.

Looking back, I now see more clearly how God sometimes places us in uncomfortable situations to stretch and mature us. During my time in Ukraine, both before my motorcycle and after, I had numerous opportunities to sit and share my life's story and be receptive to the people I talked to. If you're like me, you get caught up in the "go, go, go" mentality of everyday life and sometimes forget what's truly important. As I read the Bible, I don't see Jesus taking the quick route to where He was going. Often, I see Jesus going out of His way towards someone in need. He put other's needs above His, and it seemed to be intentional. I understand Jesus didn't live in a time of city buses and motorcycles, but I have a strong feeling that if He had, he would have taken the route filled with broken people who needed a shoulder to lay their head on and an ear to hear their struggles.

As you progress through life, I encourage you to slow down. Look around for those who need a helping hand and those who seem to be forgotten. It's often easy to take the quickest or least resistant route towards your destination, but as I've found, it often comes at a cost.

Some of the most meaningful and long-lasting relationships I've formed over my few short years on earth have stemmed from seemingly meaningless interactions with people who happened to be on the same path I was on. As I get older and experience more life, I look for ways to slow down, to say "hello" to the person next to me, and maybe, just maybe, allow our paths to converge, if only for a moment. Who knows, perhaps the person next to you is waiting for you to greet them, and neither of you has any idea that's the case.

After giving up my motorcycle, I saw God reaching towards me in a gentle and unassuming way when I wasn't in a hurry to get anywhere. I think many of us live our lives waiting for someone to reach out to us, but we often fill our time and thoughts with distractions that prevent those connections. We live our lives in constant anticipation of "today's problems" or "the next thing" and don't slow down enough to zoom out and realize there's a much larger picture in front of us.

My hope for myself, and for you, is that we can learn to take the slower route towards our destination if it allows our hearts to connect with those around us. Be careful to not let your heart have only one seat like my motorcycle did. If that's you, trade it in for a bus ticket and a bunch of strangers that will help you grow in love. You won't regret it.

Dear University,

I used to think I had to take someone else's path towards my destination. Now I know I can carve my own journey.

As my time in Ukraine came to a close, I began considering the next steps in my life. Part of me wanted to continue my adventure in Ukraine, and other parts of me wanted to find an entirely new place to experience. Despite my adventure abroad, I wanted to graduate from college and decided to pursue that objective after being accepted to the University of Alabama. I saw my acceptance as a sign of my future and decided to commit myself to accomplish the goal of graduating.

From speaking with friends who were already at the university, I knew the school's administration required certain things of their incoming freshmen students. Some of the items on their list were simple and helpful, like attending a school tour. Others, like living on campus in a dorm under university employees' supervision, seemed like a waste of time for someone who had lived overseas. Whether I was right or wrong, I felt I had a shot at being exempt from a few of their policies if I explained my situation in a letter to them.

My letter started like any other. I introduced myself and addressed the reason for my letter in the first place. I made clear from the beginning I intended to be exempt from some of their requirements, but I wanted the person reading the letter to understand why. I didn't want to come across as a snotty-nosed kid who didn't want to follow their rules. Still, I did want them to know I may have already accomplished a few of the intended outcomes their rules pointed new students towards.

I started from the beginning of my journey to Ukraine. I told the university about how I had graduated high school with a big dream and found a way to see it through. I explained the frustrations and joys I experienced in my school's hallways as I wrestled with my peers and teachers, convincing them to take my aspirations seriously. I expressed the self-doubt and criticism I faced while choosing a path less traveled. I wanted the university to know I had learned not to give up on my dreams. When I started my journey, I understood my goal and made it my mission to not give up on achieving it.

I explained how the fountain pen and blank journals gifted to me as I embarked on my adventure in Ukraine started a new way of thinking for me. With a pen and paper in hand, my days of living abroad fueled a careful and anticipatory outlook on life. Due to my time overseas, I looked at the world with wonder and expectation of something worth capturing and remembering. Surely college would provide enough content worth remembering and contemplating, and I was now better prepared to capitalize on those moments.

As my letter progressed, I explained how I had been the new guy in town before and how I had learned to operate in a foreign country with much less supervision than the university could provide me in a dorm. I had navigated people old and young, poor and destitute, drunk and mentally unstable during my adventure in Ukraine. On top of that, I added, I didn't have the luxury of using my native language. I reasoned I could likely find a way to learn the ropes in a college town by myself if they'd trust me to.

I expressed my understanding of how college is often a time of social expansion and learning how to navigate conversations with people from all walks of life. I let the university in on my experience with a few drunk Ukrainian hairdressers and angry policemen on a train too. I figured most kids my age hadn't been in a position of panic and discomfort while facing the possibility of being arrested in a foreign country for a crime they didn't commit. Ukraine had taught me a thing or two about dealing with people different than myself, and I was thankful for that.

My college years were sure to provide times of questioning, feelings of hopelessness, and a certain amount of fear. Just like the time I wandered the isles of the Ukrainian grocery store by myself, I was bound to feel lost again. In my early days in Ukraine, the grocery store taught me humility, patience, and the will to figure things out. I was looking forward to using those skills throughout college.

I imagined the university didn't just have personal responsibility lessons in mind, but likely the students' safety as well. I had walked through college buildings before, and I remembered seeing signs with instructions for a fire escape plan by each of the doors. I thought it was fitting to share my story about the massive wildfires I had experienced in my village and how I had learned life-long lessons then. It was demonstrated to me then how being prepared for any event, and having the ability to react to anything thrown my way, was important.

College was sure to test my commitment to hard work and fighting when times got tough. Thankfully, the time I spent swinging an axe in Ukraine taught me that even when I face setbacks, it's worthwhile to push through and accomplish my goal. There were sure to be difficult moments during college, and things wouldn't go the way I wanted them to, but Ukraine had taught me how to remain steadfast. I doubted college would give me splinters or require self-administered surgery, but just like people at camp in Ukraine depended on Team Hot Water for a warm shower, I was attending college in preparation for a family who would one day depend on me to provide even more.

I'm sure it was low on their list of concerns, but I also included my stories about strange cats and cows and how I was sure I could find a way to feed myself. Some of the university officials may have understood how a college kid's diet of Ramen noodles and frozen pizza isn't always nutritious, but I wanted them to know that for me, it might be a step up. If I had found a way to survive on the questionable things I had on my plate in Ukraine, I thought I'd be just fine feeding myself in college.

During my time abroad, I met some truly incredible people who extended a helping hand towards me. In turn, I also met some people who needed a second chance and a reminder that they had undeniable self-worth. I wanted the university to know I had already begun my life-long discovery of the value of people and how I should always be looking to help someone other than myself. Because Mr. Tony had quietly provided an example of putting others' needs before his own, I was now better equipped to consider someone else before myself.

I had also already been introduced to the freedoms that come with navigating around town on my own accord. The freedom to move about as I saw fit was not new to me, but my motorcycle in Ukraine had taught me something. The question for me wasn't whether I'd run wild around campus; instead, the growing knowledge in my head and heart was centered around investing in the people around me. Ukraine had taught me it's alright to be still. In fact, I had learned it's sometimes advisable to slow down and get to know the people around me on a deeper and more meaningful level.

Just like any other time in my life, sadness and doubt would pop up from time to time. I learned this first hand sitting in Steven's freezing kitchen on New Year's Eve in Ukraine. I had already felt what it means to be lonely and uncomfortable. I missed people back home and knew the feelings I had were only momentary on that winter day. College was sure to provide instances of the same feelings, but I had been through it before. I now had a roadmap to get me out.

Ukraine taught me how to look on the brighter side of things and see my emotions as fuel to help someone else. I knew when I began to feel lonely, confused, or depressed, I would remember how to look at myself in a window's reflection and find a way forward just as I had done in Steven's kitchen. After all, if I felt the way I did while looking out of his kitchen window on a cold January night, someone else was sure to be feeling the same way and probably for better reasons. I was now more aware and eager to spot people in the same emotional place I was that night, and I was more equipped to help them now. Just like the village men trying to welcome a few trouble makers in a black BMW, I now looked for people to provide an open heart and outstretched hand.

After many edits of my letter to the university, I once again sealed my hopes in an envelope and dropped them in the mail. I memorized when the mail ran and waited by the mailbox each day. Just like the letters I sent at the start of my adventure in Ukraine, I waited weeks before receiving a reply. As my confidence in getting a reply began to dwindle, the mailman delivered an envelope addressed to me from the University of Alabama.

Not only was I admitted to the school, but I also received a personalized response to the letter I had sent the administration. To my surprise, the university saw something in me and excused me from all freshmen obligations regarding on-campus living and introductory programs. To be fair, what they were excusing me from wasn't life-altering. Still, the idea behind my exemption was what captured my attention. When the university administration agreed to allow me to bypass their freshmen requirements, they also told me they believed in me and validated some of the lessons Ukraine had taught me.

Now, many years after moving back from Ukraine and graduating from college, I look back on my years overseas with ever-increasing fondness. I see myself at seventeen years old, a skinny kid with long hair and a one-way ticket to an adventure, and I still smile. I remember the idealistic outlook of life's possibilities Ukraine instilled in me, and I come alive. I also get excited knowing there's someone else out there ready to take the leap into living on the edge of their seat. Maybe a few of my words will help you do just that.

As the years go by, we all get more responsibilities, and our time seems to be stretched thinner. My hope in writing this book is to remind you, and myself, that we have what it takes to do something extraordinary. God has given each of us unique gifts, outlooks, and desires to be used for His glory. Whether you are a high school kid with a big dream or an adult with a kid's heart for exploration, adventure, and whimsy, I hope you know you have what it takes to get out there and do "*it*."

Don't ignore the "thing" God has placed in your heart. It's there for a reason. If you're like me, it's easy to fall into the trap of suppressing certain ideas or goals. They seem too outlandish, too reckless, or too scary. It's alright to have these thoughts; just don't let them stand in the doorway that leads to seeing your "thing" come to life. None of us are getting any younger, but we can all continue to become braver, more childlike in our faith, and more willing to live life to the fullest.

If you haven't already, I encourage you to write down a list of ideas and adventures you have for the rest of your life. Ask yourself how you want to spend your time, what you want to accomplish and who you want to impact. We will all be remembered by the things we did, not the things we wished we had done. Hope is a good thing, but hope without action is just a dream.

With your list in hand, commit to sharing it with who you care most about. My guess is if you let them in on your passions and ideas, they will be your biggest supporters and encouragers. You'll have days of doubt, and you'll certainly take a few wrong turns, but that's alright. On the days you feel the most discouraged, pull your list back out and remember the reason for your journey. Don't let the disbelievers, the mundane, or those who simply want to see you fail out of spite hold you down. Commit yourself to living life in a meaningful and worthwhile way, and don't look back. You have what it takes.

Now, get after it.

Epilogue

A year after moving back from Ukraine and beginning college, I found myself at a confusing junction. I had my adventure of living in Ukraine behind me, and I now had a year of college under my belt. I knew the path I was on towards a degree was one I wanted to continue, but I still strongly felt the familiar pull to Ukraine. As summer approached between my freshman and sophomore years at the University of Alabama, I spent a lot of time sitting quietly and considering the next steps in my life.

Ukraine was at the top of my list until I met a girl named Hannah one day in May. As you know from previous mentions of her, Hannah became my wife four years after I met her on a random early summer evening. Our meeting was by accident. I had chosen to spend a few hours with a friend at a local Starbucks to discuss life's possibilities. In fact, the friend I was with is one of the guys I still take an annual trip with to a national park with the sole intention to risk failure and discomfort.

It wasn't my intention to meet anyone new, especially my future wife. Just two weeks before my introduction to Hannah, I had a candid conversation with my mother about my lack of desire to marry any time in the near future. At the time, I saw the things I wanted to do with my life, and I didn't see a woman beside me in my pursuit of those things. I didn't yet know having a woman like Hannah around is exactly what I needed.

When I met Hannah, my eyes were fixed on world travel, adventures larger than my hometown, and people groups far beyond my zip code. When I first saw Hannah, I had recently moved back from Ukraine, and I was in the planning stages of making Ukraine my home again for at least the next summer. I was a student at the University of Alabama, but I saw my summers as a time to continue what I had started in Ukraine just a short time before.

I didn't see the need for a life-long companion, and I wasn't too interested in searching for someone to give my last name to. To be fair, I didn't have people knocking down my door for marriage either. Regardless, I didn't have a conceivable way of saving up for a fancy ring even if I had met someone special. But, I think that was just an excuse I stored away in case I met someone extraordinary.

At this point in my life, I had already experienced a life-changing experience while living abroad. Ukraine had become a passion, and I knew I'd find myself within its borders soon again, even if for just a short time. The things I had encountered in Ukraine felt too real to throw away, and I didn't want to deal with my heart being pulled in two seemingly different directions. On the one hand, I wanted to commit myself to a life in pursuit of loving others who were vastly different than me. On the other, I understood joining my life's dreams and goals with another human remained a worthwhile possibility. I didn't yet know I could have both outcomes if only I met the right woman.

Regardless of my thoughts and feelings, it became apparent God had a different idea of my future. As I sat outside of my local Starbucks, slumped too far into my chair to appear even remotely approachable, Hannah appeared as she stepped out of her red Ford Mustang. She was wearing a white top and jean shorts on the warm summer night, and I thought she looked like someone out of a movie. I don't imagine I looked inconspicuous doing so, but I quickly sat up straight and adjusted my wrinkled button-up shirt with the hope of her noticing me. She was way out of my league, but I figured I'd put forth my best effort to look attractive on the off-chance I was her type.

My friend and I sat there for hours, continuing to talk as I gave not so subtle glances in Hannah's direction. She argues this point, but I don't remember ever seeing my glances reciprocated. As the night went on, I didn't think the person in front of me would become more than a memory of an attractive girl at a coffee shop. My mind was still in a place of longing for a life filled with ideas and goals that didn't necessitate a life-long supporter and friend.

As my conversation wrapped up with the friend I was with, he mentioned he knew the girl's name who had captured my attention. He explained he had known of her years before from church, but he had never spoken with her. "Hannah is her name," he said, "but I don't know her last name." With all of the girls named "Hannah" in the world, I didn't think there was a great shot at ever knowing her last name either.

I'd come to find out later one of Hannah's friends also knew my first name, but not my last. I guess that's how things go in a small town like the one I grew up in. After a few awkward messages on Facebook, Hannah and I exchanged phone numbers and decided to meet with a group of friends the next night. The plan was to meet at a nearby park that had sand volleyball courts and play my friends against hers.

Rain began to fall just after we all stepped onto the court, and our plans were canceled. I didn't know it at the time, but the Lord had carved out a path for me towards a lasting relationship with Hannah that night because I later discovered she was a star volleyball player at her high school. To put it nicely, I did not share this trait with her, and it would have shown if we had been able to play that night. The Lord knew my pride could only take a few volleys and spared it even before the first serve.

Instead of playing volleyball, all of our friends split, and I found myself at Hannah's parents' house. In all my wisdom and forethought, I decided not to bring shoes with me that night. In my young mind, I had not considered the need for shoes beyond the sand volleyball court and simply left them at home. The reality of needing shoes hit me when I was standing at the threshold of Hannah's childhood home with sandy feet as I shook her father's hand for the first time.

Luckily, Hannah's parents welcomed me without mention of the sand I tracked throughout their house. I was thankful for this because their living room looked similar to the sandy courts we had just come from after I walked through. After a few pleasantries, Hannah excused us to a separate room where we sat across from one another. Being an introvert, I was never a lady's man or someone who would make a teenage daughter's father uncomfortable. I was reserved and polite, and I was content with learning more about Hannah as we talked.

After four hours of discussing where we'd come from and where we were headed, I said goodnight to Hannah as I walked out the same door I had entered. I knew another conversation with my mother would be in order as I left Hannah's parents' house that night, but I didn't want to admit it just yet. I was confused by how a girl could have a radical impact on my life's trajectory after only one conversation, but I knew something had happened deep within me. I was energetic but also confused.

A month after meeting Hannah, I was bound again for Ukraine. The friend I had been at Starbucks with shared the same affection for Ukraine and its people, and we had decided to spend another summer abroad with local orphans. We didn't have world-changing plans, but we knew we had something to offer a bunch of kids who didn't know what the word "love" meant. Despite my growing interest in Hannah, I knew my passion for Ukraine and its people was still blossoming in my heart.

In our years of dating, Hannah knew my passion for Ukraine and was kind enough not to stand in the way of my dreams. She didn't make ultimatums of "her" versus "them," she simply said, "Follow your heart." I think a lot of people say similar phrases with an anticipatory tone, which suggests the only correct answer is the one they've chosen, but Hannah never presented her desires in this way. Her desire for my joy and fulfillment has never been muddled by the notion of having to choose the "right" path. She simply looks towards me and smiles as I discover what I want in life. I have never questioned Hannah's sincerity, but I also know she is never without a plan.

When the time came for the all-too-familiar airport hugs followed by the silent study of the back of my retreating self, Hannah stood confident, trusting God would bring us back together in His timing. As I made the pivot towards my awaiting plane, she slipped me a stack of envelopes held together by interlocked twine. Each envelope simply had a number on the front, one for each week I planned to be away in Ukraine. There were five in total.

At the time, I didn't understand the significance of what Hannah had given me. On the one hand, it was a stack of envelopes sequentially numbered, but on the other, it was a gesture signifying her willingness to wait for something more meaningful. She was willing to put the work in to realize a relationship bound for something beyond its current state. That sort of gesture was exactly what I needed to move beyond my stubborn mindset.

For the next five weeks, I went about my days in Ukraine as I had done when I lived there full-time. Each day was filled with showing little orphaned kids they had a greater purpose in life, and telling how God looks towards them with adoration and love. As before, my time with the forgotten kids of Ukraine proved to be impactful and enduring in my life. My desire was to see a redemptive change in them. I continually prayed for and sought to be the catalyst for God to initiate a forever transformation in their young hearts. Little did Hannah know at the time, she was also changing my heart and affections for something life-long and restorative.

Just like before, my time in Ukraine was mostly spent in remote villages far away from modern conveniences. Every act was deliberate, and each need of those I was serving was catered to. As I've mentioned before, getting groceries was a task fit for a day's work, and communicating with people outside the bubble I lived in was equally a challenge. I didn't have the luxury of sending a quick text message or social media post. Each act of connecting with people outside the village was met with obstacles that required careful planning to overcome.

Hannah's letters stirred an emotion and desire in my heart that superseded rational thought. Each letter was a reminder of our growing relationship, and I desperately wanted to communicate with her. The saying "distance makes the heart grow fonder" must be true because the distance between Hannah and I felt measurable in the worst way possible. The fact I was in an old Soviet-built village in Eastern Ukraine while she was 5500 miles away in America felt palpable and real. Regardless of the challenges opposing our communication, I knew I had to figure out how to connect with the person at the other end of the string tugging at my heart.

I knew accessing the Internet was a task fit for a day's work from my previous time in Ukraine. Doing so would mean a few early mornings and bus rides into the city with fingers crossed the connection would be fast enough to see Hannah's face on my screen. Without drawing attention to myself, I jotted down the bus routes that would take me to an Internet cafe in the city and boarded a bus headed in that direction at my first opportunity. I understood my previous interactions with public transit would offer a chance to interact with locals, and I became doubly excited for my trip from the village to the city.

As my first chance of making a break for the city approached, I began to feel excited and anxious. It had been a couple of weeks since I last spoke with Hannah, and I had a lot to tell her. I wanted to catch her up on what I was doing in Ukraine, but I also wanted to hear about what was going on in her life. Secretly, I wanted to know if she still thought about me, but I figured her feelings would be self-evident in the way she communicated with me.

It was an early Saturday morning when I finally got the chance to escape from the village I was living in. I had memorized the bus route that would deliver me to a conversation with Hannah. I'm not a morning person, but I was up earlier than necessary for the opportunity to speak with Hannah. After I jumped out of bed, I scurried over to my friend's bed and woke him up for the adventure which awaited us. He was a bit more groggy and slow-moving, but he was excited about the significance of our trip as well.

After several hours of bumping and bouncing around on the bus, we eventually arrived at our destination in the city. Our final goal was only a few hundred yards away, and I could see a depiction of a computer signifying Internet access on the sign of the business. Again, I moved a bit quicker than my friend, but we made it to our renewed sense of civilization together. During the bus ride, I reviewed the letters Hannah had written to me. I looked for cues in her word choice and punctuation. I wanted to be sure I understood her intentions and feelings correctly. My nightmare was I'd misunderstand her words and gestures for something more than what she had intended.

Once I sat down in the Internet cafe with my computer in front of me, I paid the modest one Dollar price to access the Internet and awaited Hannah's arrival. Given our distance, she was a full eight hours behind my time, which meant she had to wake up in the middle of the night to talk with me. She had set a few alarms on her cell phone to be sure she didn't miss our chat.

As the Internet connected Hannah and me, her face appeared in front of me on my computer screen. Her image was delayed, and her movements bounced around sporadically. I could see her smiling, but her voice broke in a digital delay. We could see each other, but our voices couldn't convey the words we wanted to say.

After a few frustrating minutes, we resorted to typing our conversation while looking at each other's glitching images. Finally, Hannah and I were communicating in real-time, even if we had to battle a slow Internet connection. All of the ideas we wanted to express to each other in our dating relationship were now possible, and I was over-joyed. Just a few weeks before, I had been content with figuring life out on my own, but now, I sat face-to-face with the woman who held my heart.

Although I couldn't find the words to express what I was beginning to feel for Hannah, it was apparent we were growing closer. My affections for her were met in equal parts, and I understood my notion of a single-headed approach to life had expired. God had placed a woman before me who enveloped a keen sense of love and care which I had yet to experience in life. Hannah's purposeful approach to my heart had resulted in an undeniable reckoning with what Christ meant for an earthly bond between man and woman.

Several years after reclaiming America as my home, Hannah and I married on a hot summer day at the end of June. All of our friends and family were present to witness us commit the rest of our lives to each other. In that sacred moment, she and I confessed we would stand by each other in the best and worst of times and fight for each other regardless of the outcome. Our dreams and ambitions became one, and our future experiences became a predetermined agreement that we'd put the other before ourselves.

As I examine the bond Hannah and I now share, I am forced to compare it to what Christ has promised His children. I don't think God accidentally put Hannah and me in the position of a relentless pursuit of one another when it came to our blossoming relationship. When I look back towards my agreement with God, I see Him choosing to pursue me in the same way Hannah and I sought after each other. There was no amount of space, time, or less-than-ideal circumstances that would have allowed God not to reach me. He wanted my heart when He first made me, and He still wants it today.

Throughout our marriage, I have always known Hannah to be thoughtful and kind. She has continuously reminded me of what it means to chase after something greater than the "here and now." Despite my wandering heart for adventure, she grounds me in the loving remembrance that Christ is enough. In the times I begin to wonder, she pulls me back to placing my hope and trust in Jesus, knowing all will work out for His glory and my satisfaction. I have a small Russian sign on my desk from Hannah that says, "It's not the amount of days in your life, it's the amount of life in your days." Hannah has faithfully proven this to be true, and I thank God He was gracious enough to give me someone who continually points me to Him and towards a life filled with purpose.

Many years have gone by since I moved back from Ukraine, but my desire to find joy and adventure while loving those around me hasn't waned. I look back at my time living in Ukraine, the visits back, and saying "I do" to Hannah as building blocks in my life. Each period signifies a deep change within me and a shift in perspective as I continue to look at the world with awe and a sense of adventure. I still have big dreams, and I'm more inclined now to not give credence to the voices that tell me "no." The lessons I've chronicled in this book have filled me with renewed confidence and aspiration to follow my wildest dreams. I hope my words have done the same for you.

As Hannah and I progress in our lives and marriage, we continue to desire to reach young hearts and minds. Our eyes are constantly open to ways we can reach and influence people who have crazy dreams. We strive to be the helping hand in your journey and pray the Lord will continue to allow us to do just that. Together, we're a team pursuing young adults who look at the world and see whimsy and adventure. We figure if we can encourage just one person to chase after their dreams, our efforts will have been well worth it. Let us know if we can help you.

Acknowledgments

*Just like in this book, some of the names below have been changed to protect the identity of those mentioned. Those of you mentioned using a fake name will easily be able to decode my gratitude below. Please don't allow your name change to devalue my sincere appreciation for all you've done for me.

I can't help but to publicly thank my wife, Hannah, for her contributions to making this book come to life. Without her patient reviews of countless edits, this book would have been printed in an unreadable form. Beyond her attention to detail and willingness to read this book many times, she has consistently encouraged me to finish writing so I can get this book into your hands.

Mom and Dad, thank you for taking a chance and letting me move half-way across the world at seventeen. I'm still not sure if my moving away was a present to you, but nonetheless, thanks for believing in me and supporting me.

Adam and Charlotte, thank you for opening your home and family in Ukraine. As I have a home and family of my own now, I better understand the sacrifices you made for me. I can't thank you enough for your patience, love, and direction while I lived with you in Ukraine.

Steven, your apartment became a refuge of sorts throughout my stay in Ukraine. Your friendship, guitar playing/singing, and hospitality made me feel special and I can't thank you enough.

To the family whose adoption process I shadowed, thank you for your friendship and generosity. You allowed me to stay with you for weeks on end and paid for a lot of my meals. Thank you, also, for introducing me to Adam and Charlotte and providing the opportunity for me to ask them for a key to their house.

Jay, your incredibly thoughtful gift of a custom pen and journal served as the catalyst for this project. Without your gift, I'm not sure I would have written this book. I wish I could tell you in person here on Earth, but I'll see you again one day and tell you then.

Michael, thank you for being gracious and professional in formatting my manuscript. You made my words look like a real book, and I can't thank you enough.

Katarina, thank you for designing and formatting my book cover. You too were professional and kind.

Cameron, not only did you provide the photo of me for this book, but you also came to visit me when I was living in Ukraine. Your spontaneity and friendship mean a lot to me, and I'm thankful you agreed to allow me to use a photo you took.

Lastly, thank you to all of you who either prayed or financially donated to my adventure in Ukraine. Without you, and your support, I would have never been able to chase the wild idea that now fills these pages. I hope this book brings you joy.

Made in the USA
Monee, IL
28 February 2022

92018833R00121